BIDDING TO BUY

A STEP-BY-STEP GUIDE TO INVESTING IN REAL ESTATE FORECLOSURES

DAVID OSBORN
AARON AMUCHASTEGUI

BiggerPockets®
PUBLISHING
Denver, Colorado

Praise for David Osborn's Books

"When it comes to all the tools that David and Paul deliver as they play to win on the road to financial freedom, 'abundance' may be an understatement. Their passion for entrepreneurship and commitment to supporting their global community add depth to their success strategies for 'life at the top' and the messages of inspiration in *Wealth Can't Wait*."

—Robert Kiyosaki, Entrepreneur, educator, and author of *Rich Dad Poor Dad*

"Osborn and Morris offer their approach to building a successful business and building wealth. There is a lot of information packed into the book, and yet it remains an engaging and accessible read."

—Caroline Ceniza-Levine, Senior Contributor at Forbes.com

"If you've struggled to make change, or it seems like you've done everything right and something still seems wrong, my bet is that you're disconnected from the fundamental truth that who you surround yourself with determines your future. Your opportunity to rediscover that truth—and change your life—lies in this remarkable story."

—Hal Elrod, Author of the *New York Times* bestseller *The Miracle Morning* and *The Miracle Equation*

"A wonderful story and a compelling guide to why surrounding yourself with the right people is so important to success."

—Jeff Hoffman, Serial entrepreneur and Co-founder of Priceline.com

BIDDING TO BUY
A STEP-BY-STEP GUIDE TO INVESTING IN REAL ESTATE FORECLOSURES

Praise for
Aaron Amuchastegui's Books

"*The 5-Hour School Week* is the guide that will show you how to identify the best educational model for your family. Highly recommended."

**—Hal Elrod, International
Bestselling Author of *The Miracle Morning***

"Homeschooling provides an unrivaled opportunity to develop a growth mindset for our kids, and *The 5-Hour School Week* is a great example of that very reality. Aaron and Kaleena have put together a must-read manifesto for any family, whether you homeschool now or are thinking of it for the future."

**—Matt Beaudreau, Founder of
Acton Roseville and Keynote Speaker**

"Allow this book to bring you encouragement, inspiration, and some practical how-tos. As a homeschooler myself, I'm walking away from reading this book with a fresh perspective on our journey and can't wait to start implementing our own 5-hour school week!"

**—Lindsay and Mike McCarthy, Co-author of *The Miracle
Morning* for Parents and Families, and
CEO of Gobundance and Fambundance**

"*The 5-Hour School Week* focuses on the most important lessons and implements them by following the child—an art most of society has lost."

**—Jim and Jamie Sheils, Bestselling Author of *The Family
Board Meeting*, and Co-creators of the Education Matrix
and the 18 Summers Movement**

Bidding to Buy: A Step-by-Step Guide to Investing in Real Estate Foreclosures
David Osborn and Aaron Amuchastegui

Published by BiggerPockets Publishing LLC, Denver, Colorado
Copyright © 2020 by David Osborn and Aaron Amuchastegui
All Rights Reserved.

Publisher's Cataloging-in-Publication Data
Names: Osborn, David, author. | Amuchastegui, Aaron, author.
Title: Bidding to buy : a step-by-step guide to investing in real estate foreclosures / by David Osborn and
Aaron Amuchastegui.
Description: Includes bibliographical references. | Denver, CO: BiggerPockets Publishing, 2020.
Identifiers: LCCN: 2020936055 | ISBN: 9781947200333 (pbk.) | 9781947200340 (ebook)
Subjects: LCSH Real estate investment--United States. | Foreclosure--United States. | House buying--
United States. | Investments. | BISAC BUSINESS & ECONOMICS / Real Estate / Buying & Selling Homes |
BUSINESS & ECONOMICS / Investments & Securities / Real Estate | BUSINESS & ECONOMICS / Real
Estate / General
Classification: LCC HD255 .O79 2020 | DDC 332.63/24--dc23

Published in the United States of America and printed on recycled paper.
10 9 8 7 6 5 4 3 2 1

TABLE OF CONTENTS

PART II
The Five Steps

INTRODUCTION
PART I
Love, Foreclosures, and the Freedom to Choose

On the surface, this looks like a book about real estate.

Specifically, it looks like a book about one type of real estate investment that for both me and my co-author, Aaron—as well as thousands of others—has been incredibly rewarding.

But that's just on the surface. What lies underneath is more like a love letter—a testament to our unwavering belief that real estate is the greatest tool in history for not only building wealth but taking control of your life.

Believe me, I know. Starting out broke and unemployed at age 26, I had begun selling homes simply because I had to do *something*. I was a C student with an uneven track record and only the murkiest idea of where I was headed. Yet, ten years later, I went on to build one of the top real estate brokerages in the world.

For me, real estate checked every box. It was safe, it gave me leverage, it provided cash flow. If nothing else, I could drive by a house I owned and just *look* at it. Heck, I could move in if I really had to.

At some point, I made the mistake of thinking I could do the same thing in the stock market. And for a while, it seemed like I could; my portfolio kept climbing in value, and the only downside seemed to be kicking myself for all the market years I'd missed out on.

That is, until I lost it all. Not long after my fist-pumping, high-flying success, the market tanked and so did my net worth.

I was shattered. That had never happened to me in real estate. Sure, the housing market was cyclical, like everything else, but through careful buying, I had cash coming in even during down times. Better still, I had real assets I could see and touch.

It was now painfully clear that I couldn't say that about stocks. I realized that, for me, they were just numbers on a screen. I knew they were assets, but I couldn't internalize them. I couldn't fall in love with stocks the way I had with real estate.

So I dusted myself off and doubled down on what I knew to be true. Less than a decade later, I found a new love. It was still real estate, but now I was buying foreclosures—hundreds at a time. The numbers were huge, but at the end of the day, I could still drive past any one of those homes and say, "Yup. Still there."

Since then, I've never looked back. To this day, the vast majority of my wealth is real estate-related. I love it, plain and simple.

To be clear, it's not the money I love. That's only a means to a much more important end: the freedom to do the things I choose with the people I love. A nine-to-five job can't give me that freedom, and it won't give you that freedom either. For that, you need to be in business.

You could start a tech company. You could become a restaurateur. You could open a retail store or a factory. The sky's the limit.

Of all the possibilities, however, real estate is the simplest business I know of. You get to buy something of value and then immediately use it to make money. You don't need a staff. You don't have to build products or open a store. You buy a house, rent it out, and *voilà*: you're in business.

Try doing that with a restaurant or a tech company.

The foreclosure business is like a machine for making money, but you get to see exactly how the machine works. There are no hidden parts. There's no mystery.

Foreclosures also shine in one special area. They offer you all the advantages of real estate with one more game-changing bonus: You get to buy at a discount.

That's big. Ask any investor or entrepreneur what the secret to building wealth is, and invariably their answers will lead you back to something that rests on the idea of buying at a discount: Buy low, sell high. Never lose money. Lock in your margin. Build in a safety moat.

Buying real estate at a discount gives you options like no other investment. Your costs are lower. You have cash flow.

That is the real story of buying foreclosures on the courthouse steps. It's a chance to create a near-instant business with a safety margin, one that can start delivering cash back to you almost immediately. Meanwhile, someone else is paying for that business. And when you're done with it, there's a bunch of people standing in line to buy it from you.

That's what I love, and that's why this isn't just a book about real estate; it's a book about freedom, about taking control of your life and living it the way you want to.

There is, of course, a caveat. It would be easy to read this and think foreclosures are foolproof. They aren't. Real estate is simple, but it's not always easy. To manage risk, I've relied on the single most powerful tool in my kit: discipline. I've bought thousands of homes, and for all of them, I've used a system. I've used a system to find them, a system to analyze them and choose the best ones, and a system to buy them.

This book is about a reliable method not just for buying real estate but for moving a little bit closer to true freedom every day.

How could you *not* fall in love with an investment like that?

Thanks for joining us on this journey.

—David Osborn
New York Times best-selling author of *Wealth Can't Wait*

INTRODUCTION
PART II

Finding Profits on the Courthouse Steps

In 2009, I was going out of business.

That might sound like an event, but going out of business is a *process*. It takes time—painful, slow-motion, can't-sleep-at-night time.

My partners and I were home builders, which was a great business to be in...until it wasn't. After the housing crash, everything changed and we were left worrying about how to make payroll and pay the bills.

Watching our business dry up did leave us with more time, and we used it to do what any true entrepreneur does when facing failure: look for a *new* business. That may sound crazy, but as you'll learn, falling in love with difficult problems is a kind of superpower. With any luck, by the end of what follows, it will be your superpower too.

We had heard of people who were making money by flipping foreclosures. I was skeptical—it had a vague, get-rich-quick feel to it. Still, it was related to the skills and experience we had, and I thought it was worth looking into. It was certainly better than feeling powerless as our business slowly evaporated.

The people we knew were finding homes listed on our local MLS, or multiple listing service—a database of properties for sale. The idea was simple enough: find a home that someone had stopped making payments on, buy it cheap, then fix it up and resell it for a higher price.

What, we thought, could be any easier? After all, we were home builders. We were experts at this kind of thing. How hard could it be?

Harder than we thought.

We spent hours, then days, then *weeks* trying to buy foreclosed properties through MLS listings. There were five of us, and we wrote *hundreds* of offers. We made offers with no conditions. We made offers in cash. We did everything we could think of that you would normally do to buy a damn house on the MLS.

Not one offer was accepted.

A Different Kind of Foreclosure Listing

At the time, *foreclosure* was a word we were hearing a lot. It was 2009, and people were losing their homes every day. Still, we had only the most basic understanding of what foreclosure meant and how it worked. As we understood it, when someone stopped making their mortgage payments, the bank eventually took possession of their home. That meant the loan had been "foreclosed on," and the homeowner lost their property to the lender.

That was essentially true, but it didn't explain why we couldn't seem to *buy* one of those houses people had stopped paying for. We were utterly confused.

What we didn't realize at the time was that we were trying to buy homes *in the wrong place*. Not "place" as in geography but "place" as in the wrong point in the timeline of the foreclosure process.

When a foreclosure is listed by a Realtor on the MLS, *anyone* can see it, and they can do so from the comfort of their home. The MLS is where everyone is looking. The competition for properties is high, and as we soon realized, the Realtors listing those properties already had preferred clients they were working with. We simply couldn't find our way in.

We had no idea there was a whole different arena for foreclosure sales—places where properties were bought before they ever made it out into the wider public eye.

The *Aha!* Moment

As luck would have it, one of my partners discovered that a property right beside his was listed for foreclosure. Curious, we tried to find out more, but the property was nowhere to be found on the MLS—it wasn't online *anywhere*. The only information we had to work with was the physical foreclosure notice at the home itself. It listed a date when the property would be sold at *auction* and an address where the sale would happen.

The address turned out to be the local courthouse.

That was when the lightbulb went on. Suddenly it made sense. There was a whole *world* of properties being sold at auction before they were ever picked up by real estate agents or listed on the MLS! We'd been swimming in a sea of competing buyers when the real deals were happening *upstream*—they were happening earlier in the foreclosure timeline.

We went to an auction the very next day.

We weren't there to buy, just to observe. The problem was that it was difficult to tell exactly what we were seeing. It was an oddly informal process. As far as we could tell, only a couple of buyers were there, and the closest thing to someone in charge was a guy who stood there and read out a list of information.

We tried to ask how it worked, but no one really wanted to tell us. At the time, there was no how-to resource we could turn to. With only days to go until the auction on the place we'd found, we'd have to figure it out for ourselves.

I spent the next two days in the county recorder's office reading every document I could find on the property we were interested in. We did our own title searches to be confident that we knew exactly who owned the property and who was owed money for it. I read page after page of legalese.

Eventually, I decided: *We can do this.*

The Courthouse Steps

Our first auction experience was nothing short of bizarre. I still look back at it with a mix of amusement and shock.

We arrived at the courthouse at the appointed time but had no idea where to go or what to do. Instead, we just hung around the courthouse steps in a corner near the entrance. There was just us, a few other people who we assumed were also there to try to buy property, and a garbage can. That was it.

A few minutes later, I looked up to see a guy in a T-shirt and shorts roll up to us on a *skateboard*. He hopped off, pulled a laptop out of his bag, and set it on the garbage can. A moment later, he began reading off property details, and a couple of other guys began bidding.

That's all there was to it. It was as casual as stepping up to a food truck and ordering a taco.

The fifth listing of the day was the one we were interested in. Skateboard Guy read off the address, along with a few details.

"The opening bid is $215,000," he said.

There was silence. No one said anything in response to the opening bid, including me. At that point, I was still in shock that a guy who arrived by skateboard and set up his office on a garbage can was auctioning off honest-to-God houses.

"Going once," Skateboard Guy said. "Going twice..."

Our partner snapped to attention. "We'd like to bid!"

At this point, it was pretty clear we were new to the process. He said to us, "Would you like to bid a penny over?"

"Yes?" we said uncertainly.

"Do you have your cashier's checks?" he asked, making no effort to hide his skepticism.

In fact, we *did* have our checks. We'd learned early on that you have to pay in cash with the precise amount (more on that later), and we held out the envelope we had received at the bank after scraping together every dollar we could round up.

"Sold," he said.

Immediately, a *gasp* went up from the strangers around me. The same people who had just been confidently snapping up properties like they were tacos now began to stare at us and whisper.

I felt my face flush. Had we made a mistake? Had we bought a property we shouldn't have? *What had we just done?*

I could feel my heart pound as I signed over our cashier's checks.

Skateboard Guy handed me a receipt. I looked at it. It had almost no information on it—not even the address of the property that (I hoped) we had just bought!

"Is this it?" I asked.

"That's it."

"But...this is just a receipt. There's no address, no...*anything*. How do I know what we just bought?"

"Oh," he said, closing his laptop. "We don't do any of that. We don't guarantee addresses. We just sell the properties. You'll get your deed in the mail."

And with that, he hopped on his skateboard and pushed off.

I looked down at the piece of paper in my hand. As he turned the corner, I thought, *That's all the money we have.*

What had I just done?

After...Math

We spent the next two weeks in a state of near panic, my nights more sleepless than ever.

I kept thinking back to the gasps I'd heard when we bought the property. What did that *mean*? Why hadn't anyone else bid? I had just spent the last of our money on something I wasn't even sure we owned. Even if we *had* bought the property, I was now lying awake at night worrying that there was something deeply wrong with it. Had someone trashed it? Was it a burned-out shell? Was it built on an ancient cemetery?

I kept berating myself. How could I have given all our money to a guy on a skateboard?

It turned out I had worried for nothing.

Two weeks later, the deed to the property arrived in the mail. We immediately had it entered at the recorder's office. Then, just to be extra sure, we got a new title report showing that we owned the property free and clear.

All my worries about the property itself were wasted too. It was just fine, and we were able to sell it right away at a significant profit—to someone who, as we had been a few weeks earlier, was trying to buy foreclosed properties on the local MLS.

I was elated. We'd pulled it off! Not only had we made money, but we could do it *again*. We'd finally found a way into the exclusive club where properties were selling at a discount. That night I slept like a baby—an exhausted, relieved, financially solvent baby.

In the coming months we repeated that success and repeated it again, buying properties at big discounts right on the courthouse steps. There wasn't always a guy on a skateboard, but it was always exciting.

We began to refocus our investment energy almost entirely on buying at auction. We bought even more properties, discovering that we could buy them and flip them—sometimes the same *day*—or that we could keep them and rent them out. Or we could add value by fixing them up and then selling them for an even bigger profit.

It was, and still is, a thrill beyond anything else I'd experienced in real estate.

Your "Backstage Pass" to Real Estate Investment

Much of the thrill of buying at auction comes from getting more-exclusive access to properties. Buying on the courthouse steps represents the early phase of the foreclosure process. It's the backstage pass of real estate: instead of waiting in the long MLS line out on the street, you sneak past the velvet ropes and through the back door, and suddenly everything changes. Instead of being one more face in a massive crowd, you're in a small group of rock and rollers. Instead of hoping to get a seat at the back, you're already in, *and* you get the best view of the show...for less money.

That's the advantage of buying at auction: You get access to properties long before most people even know they're for sale, and at a price lower than you'd pay anywhere else.

> **The goal of this book is to give YOU that same backstage pass to the world of real estate.**

The Path Ahead

Our job in the pages that follow is to make sure you feel comfortable finding, analyzing, and bidding on your first foreclosed property, right on the courthouse steps.

To reach that goal, here are a few of the things you'll find in the chapters that follow.

- You'll learn to understand the foreclosure process, and all the distinct advantages of buying property at auction.
- You'll develop the skills to find, analyze, and select the ideal properties to bid on—those that fit *your* goals and leave you a significant financial safety margin.
- We'll walk you through every step of how to attend an auction, bid in real time, and buy a property!

Along the way, of course, we'll cover a wide range of other critical steps, like building your team, dealing with money, and managing your own mind and emotions. You'll hear stories—both good and bad!—based on our own experiences and those of other seasoned auction buyers. Best of all, you'll build the confidence to know that you can succeed at investing in foreclosures.

The Biggest Thrill in Real Estate

Buying at auction gives you the one thing that every investor wants—the opportunity to buy at a lower price. To get *value* for your money.

We've spent a lot of time in the real estate business. Together, we've bought *thousands* of properties and been involved in more transactions and real estate deals than we can count. We've had our fingers in just about every aspect of the real estate business, and one thing I can tell you for sure is this: There's nothing like buying foreclosures at auction. Nothing in real estate is as exhilarating as bidding live on a property, then walking away knowing you made a great investment.

Here's to your first profit on the courthouse steps.

—Aaron Amuchastegui, CEO of Roddy's Foreclosure Listing Service
Sacramento, CA

BIDDING TO BUY

PART I

FORTUNE FAVORS THE PREPARED

CHAPTER 1
RISK AND REWARD
How Foreclosure Works and Why it Matters

After you buy a house at auction, one of the first tasks on your list is to change the locks. You have no idea how many keys are out there or who has them. It's simply good practice.

For me, the act is also symbolic. When we change the locks, it means our diligence has paid off. We've worked the process, and the process has worked. Changing the locks is the moment when the place is officially *ours*.

I don't have to actually change the locks myself, of course, and neither will you. But in the early days, I would often do the job just to take a closer look at the place and get that little jolt of satisfaction that comes from knowing you've made a great investment.

One particular sunny California day I was doing just that, hunched over the front doorknob with a few tools, when I heard footsteps. I turned to see a man standing on the walk.

"Excuse me," he said. "We're here to do the home inspection."

"I think you might have the wrong place," I said. "We just bought this property at auction and didn't schedule one."

The man's face fell. "I'm a Realtor," he said. "My clients were trying to buy the place. A short sale."

A *short sale* occurs when the bank agrees to let a struggling owner sell a home for less than is owed on it. The homeowner gets to avoid having a foreclosure on their record, and the bank gets to avoid the hassle and uncertainty of the entire foreclosure process.

In this case, it was obvious that the short sale hadn't happened in time. The home had gone to auction, where we'd become the lucky new owners.

Still, here I was, standing face-to-face with a buyer. We'd just bought the place hours ago, but who was I to say no to the winds of fortune?

"Write up a cash offer," I told him, "and we'll look at it."

We did more than look at it; we accepted it immediately.

Two weeks later, the deed arrived in the mail, and we closed the sale.

We made $40,000, and I never got past the front door.

This story perfectly illustrates the backstage pass offered by auction sales. By entering into the foreclosure process earlier, you get access to better deals. In our case, that meant buying the property for tens of thousands of dollars less than market price. It then gave us a chance to turn around and sell it right away to someone willing to pay more.

What this story *doesn't* tell us, however, is exactly why buying at auction offers such great advantages. To understand that, it's helpful to first understand what the foreclosure process looks like.

The Foreclosure Process

Backstage real estate passes don't just fall out of the sky. If they did, everyone would have them, and they wouldn't be worth anything. To understand why buying at auction can be so effective, you need to understand what a foreclosure is, and how it works.

Foreclosure is a legal process. It's a series of events that happen over time, and it begins when someone borrows money to buy real property—often a home, but it could be another type of property, too. In this book, we speak in terms of single-family residential homes, but the principles can apply to almost any kind of real estate.

The easiest way to understand the foreclosure process is through a simple example.

Let's assume that the lender is a bank—let's call it Bankopolis—and the property in question is a residential home, lived in by the homeowner, Dave.

When Dave arranged his mortgage, he signed a contract agreeing to pay back the money he owes Bankopolis at an agreed-upon rate. Dave also used the home he was buying as *collateral*—insurance, essentially, for the bank to make sure they can still get their money back if Dave doesn't keep his promises.

Using the house as collateral means the home now has a *lien* against it, and Bankopolis has a legal right to take possession of the home if Dave doesn't make his mortgage payments.

As long as Dave keeps up his end of the bargain, everything is fine. If he misses a payment, however, things start to shift. The process and timeline vary from place to place and bank to bank, but here is an overview of what happens if Dave starts to drop the ball.

1. The First Missed Payment

One day, Dave faces an unexpected crisis: He loses his job. It's not long before he's burned through his savings, and soon he can't make the agreed-upon mortgage payment. So he doesn't.

At this point, it's not the end of the world. Many mortgages have a grace period—often ten to fifteen days. Bankopolis will likely send a letter that says, *Dave, you didn't make your payment. We need to sort this out.* If Dave simply makes the payment, all is well.

2. The Second Missed Payment

If Dave doesn't pay up, however, and he misses another payment, things move further along. Bankopolis is (a) going to start to worry, and (b) add late fees to what's owed, as outlined in the mortgage.

Now that he's more than thirty days behind on his payments, Dave is likely to find Bankopolis becoming more concerned. He'll probably get phone calls and notices.

Still, things aren't disastrous for Dave. The bank would rather get paid, and Dave would like to keep his house; both parties *really* want this to work out. If Dave pays the overdue amount (plus any fees), he's square again. His credit record may take a hit, but no one is going to take his house.

3. The Third Missed Payment (and Beyond)

But if Dave doesn't settle up, new machinery starts to grind into action. When Dave misses *another* payment—that's three—he's going to get another notice, and it's more serious.

After three to six months with no payment by Dave (the time varies, depending on Dave's mortgage, his bank, the state he lives in, and the local economy and legal system), Bankopolis is going to enter a public notice called a notice of default (NOD) or a *lis pendens* (fancy Latin for "suit pending") with the county recorder's office. That notice officially states that Dave has defaulted on his mortgage and the property is scheduled for foreclosure. The notice lists an auction date when the house will be sold.

Unless Dave settles up before the auction, his mortgage is going to be foreclosed on. That means Bankopolis is going to take possession of his home, as stated in the mortgage contract.

And Dave, of course, is going to have to move out.

Note: You can see samples of real notices of default at our resource site at **BiggerPockets.com/ForeclosureBonus**

Opportunities in the Foreclosure Timeline

This process is hard on everyone. It's tough for Dave, in particular, but it's the law.

The most important thing to note right now, however, is that it's a *process*. It takes time. And that time creates opportunities for other people—like you, for example—to help both Dave and Bankopolis.

Broadly speaking, there are two types of foreclosures—judicial and nonjudicial. Both create an opportunity for investors to buy distressed real estate. In this book, although the basic principles apply to both, we're speaking specifically about nonjudicial foreclosures, those in which a judge does *not* have to rule on whether a foreclosure can proceed. That power is given to a *trustee*, who will auction off the property.

For our purposes, there are three specific points in the foreclosure timeline where investors like you tend to get involved. Each is different, and each has its pros and cons.

1. Before the Foreclosure Auction

No one wants a foreclosure. Both the borrower and the lender are better off if things work out. In a foreclosure, both parties effectively lose something.

Because foreclosure sucks for everyone, there are any number of arrangements that can be made before the property goes to auction. That saves everyone a lot of hassle and saves the borrower a serious blemish on their credit record.

The person who approached me while I was changing the locks had been hoping to make one of those arrangements. They were trying to buy the home directly from the owner *before* the foreclosure, saving everyone the pain of going all the way.

Some companies and individuals specialize in this approach—they choose to enter early in the foreclosure process. There are advantages to this. There may be less competition, for example. Prices can be better too, and you get to help both parties avoid an expensive, painful, and longer route to auction and beyond.

We've always found, however, that it takes a tremendous amount of time and effort to identify such properties and connect with the homeowners. There's a lot of legwork—a lot of selling and deal-making Homeowners were certainly not always happy to talk to us, and even if we found one who was interested, it often didn't work out.

In the end, the reward rarely seemed to justify the investment of so much time and effort, but if you are one of those people who has the ability to pull it off, getting involved before the foreclosure auction creates the ultimate win-win for you and the seller. All said, we still focus on auction.

2. After the Foreclosure Auction

Of course, there are opportunities at the other end of the foreclosure process too—*after* properties have gone to auction.

Not every property sells on the courthouse steps. The ones that don't are repossessed by the lender, often the bank. Banks, however, aren't in the real estate management business. They like to lend money to people to buy homes, but they don't like to *own* homes for long. So when a property fails to sell at auction, the bank generally likes to find a way to sell it and get at least some of their investment back.

But banks are not Realtors. They usually want someone to help with the sale, so they get a real estate brokerage to do the job. REO, or *real estate owned*, is the label given to properties that go to auction but don't sell and are then turned over by the bank to real estate professionals.

This is how we first tried to buy properties, as I described in the introduction, but we could never seem to do a deal. Buying REO properties is easier and lower risk than buying at auction, because the bank has to pay off any liens on the home and you can fully inspect the property. As a result of those benefits, the competition is fierce.

For us, though, the reward simply wasn't there.

3. The Auction Sweet Spot

There are people who build businesses around the previous two points in the timeline and do just fine—they are legitimate ways to invest in distressed real estate.

For us, however, buying on the courthouse steps has always offered the best balance of risk and reward, the right level of competition, and the best fit for our temperament.

- Compared to buying REO properties (*after* foreclosure), auctions offer a unique advantage by giving you an entry point that's upstream of the highly competitive real estate action. By buying before the brokers and agents and mortgage brokers and lawyers get involved in the usual way, you get a chance to buy properties at a discount.
- Compared to buying *before* foreclosure, auctions offer a greater return on your time and a much more enjoyable process than knocking on the doors of homeowners who are going through one of the most difficult moments of their life.

Every point in the foreclosure timeline offers potential rewards. With each reward, of course, comes a corresponding risk. For us, buying at auction was always the best combination of both. It was the sweet spot of the foreclosure timeline.

The Risks of Buying at Auction

Buying foreclosures at auction may be thrilling, and it may be a backstage pass to real estate bargains. But there is a price to pay, and that price is uncertainty. To succeed in the business, you need to understand the risks—and their corresponding rewards—in detail.

We look at five key risks for every property.

Risk #1: List Accuracy

Although it's improving, the auction business is notoriously low-tech. Most auction notices are printed on paper and posted at courthouses or other locations. To get access to that information, most people buy foreclosure lists from a service. These services are offered by businesses that send out people to gather the printed information or search through online records, compile and digitize them, and then sell the information to potential property buyers.

The first risk you face in buying foreclosures, then, is simply the quality of the information on the list. While foreclosure listing services are legitimate, valuable businesses, they face the same challenge as any business that turns printed data into digital data: Mistakes happen. There could be typos, scanning errors, misprints. There could be a zero missing on a price, a number missing on an address. The attorney that made the posting may have entered Baker Street instead of Baker Avenue. We know people who have bought a house that wasn't *there* or bought the wrong house. Really.

That's why we always follow our five-step process—so we can find those mistakes *before* we get to auction.

Risk #2: Property Condition

If you want to buy a home sold *after* auction—an REO sale—you have the right to look inside it. You can walk through it, poke around, get it inspected, and see every detail with your own eyes.

That's not the case for homes at auction. When a house is sold at auction, the intent is that the property condition—at least on the inside—is a guess. That makes the state of the property a risk. We've bought properties only to find out that the owners who defaulted on the mortgage also trashed the place. Or ripped out and sold all the cabinets, plumbing, and fixtures. Or took a hammer to the HVAC system because they were angry at the bank.

Conversely, we've also bought properties that were *stunning* inside, complete with granite countertops and expensive trim and appliances. The point is, you can't always know for sure. Fortunately, there's a way to mitigate this risk and price it into your calculations. More on that in the chapters ahead.

Risk #3: Occupancy

Properties are either occupied or unoccupied when you buy them. A vacant property makes for a much quicker process—you can change the locks and start on any improvements almost immediately. The sooner you do that, the sooner you can resell, rent, or refinance the property.

An occupied house carries additional unknowns. Squatters, tenants, or the previous owners may be living there. Occupants can take time to evict, which slows things down. If the previous owners (who stopped making the payments, triggering the foreclosure) feel that they were wrongly foreclosed on, they can file a lawsuit against the lender. We've had houses tied up for years while the process got sorted out. In those cases, you can't take possession and get on with your plans.

Of course, existing occupants can be an upside as well. They might be the perfect tenants for your new rental property. In a later chapter, we'll look at a number of clever strategies for identifying occupancy.

Risk #4: Clear Title

It's tempting to see foreclosure as a simple process involving one person who didn't make payments on one mortgage.

In reality, there can often be more than one *lien* on a home. A lien, for our purposes, means that someone has used their home as collateral to borrow money. Each lien has a priority position. A first mortgage, for example, takes priority over a second.

Some liens are extinguished in foreclosure; others need to be paid. This is by no means a deal breaker, but it does mean we need to be informed before bidding and factor what we know (or don't) into the price. If you bid $150,000 for a home at auction, for example, there could be other liens, property taxes, or other loan fees that need to be paid.

Also, remember that technically *loans*, not properties, are foreclosed on. It is possible to buy a lien in second position at auction and still not actually own the house!

The good news? There are tools and steps to help you explore title and the financial story behind every property you buy. More on that later.

Risk #5: Valuation

The biggest risk of all, but also the biggest tool at your disposal to manage all the risks above, is valuation. That's coming up with the answer to the all-important question: *What is this property worth?*

When you don't know in advance the condition of the property, the quality of the finishes, or even the floor plan, it's hard to estimate value. Your entire reason for buying at auction is to buy for less than you would otherwise. But how much should you spend?

In truth, you never know *exactly* how much to spend. But as you'll see, you can make very educated guesses.

The Rewards of Buying at Auction

Fortunately, there are two great things about the risks of auction buying. The first is that you can manage those risks by committing to a great process. The second is that the risks deliver rewards!

Reward #1: Speed

When you buy a home in the usual way—as a property listed on the MLS, purchased through an agent—things take time. You write an offer. It gets signed back. You sign it back again. Eventually, you do a deal, but escrow might take a few weeks. The closing could be months off. You visit the lawyer. You get the keys. *Finally*, the property is yours.

When you buy at auction, all of that can happen in hours. After a successful bid, you can often change the locks that afternoon and get to work on the home.

Speed can be a disadvantage in that you don't always have as much time as you'd like to do research. For the most part, however, it's an advantage (and a thrill!) that you can do a deal and become an owner on the same day.

Reward #2: Face-to-Face Negotiations

Buying a home through the MLS generally means using an agent or a middleman of some sort. You rarely deal directly with the actual property owner, and you seldom see your competition. Offers go back and forth in writing, with one party offering, the other countering. Not only is this a clunky, time-consuming system, but the lack of transparency means you can end up bidding *against yourself*.

Auctions are different. Your competition is right there. They might be standing right beside you. The person with the power to accept the bid is right there too, even if it is a guy on a skateboard. The process is face-to-face, and the stakeholders are present. You might not know as much about the property as you would with a traditional purchase, but at least you know who the players are.

Reward #3: Property Quality

Foreclosures are associated with buying run-down or otherwise deficient properties, but that's not always the case. There are also plenty of beautiful homes owned by people who simply couldn't make the payments. There are properties owned by military families who have been restationed too quickly to sell. There are people who, for reasons known only to them, simply changed their minds and walked away.

Whatever the reason for the foreclosure, there are few experiences in real estate as exhilarating as opening the door on a house you just bought and discovering that it's *beautiful*. It's well-designed, expensively appointed, and immaculately clean.

They aren't all that way, but it happens.

Reward #4: Helping

Buying at foreclosure also gets a bad rap due to its supposed impact on the property's community. In our experience, this is completely unjustified. Buying a foreclosed home is often a big help to the neighborhood. Neighbors love it when we take a boarded-up house with a lawn full of tall weeds and turn it back into something that creates value for everyone.

It might also surprise you to know that sometimes you're helping the homeowner who was foreclosed on! Occasionally, the owner is still in the home when we buy it. In those cases, they might become the new tenants. It's never nice to be foreclosed on, but we've received letters of thanks from people who have been able to stay in their homes even after losing ownership.

Reward #5: Your Own Home

Most people aren't buying foreclosures for themselves, but I have met people at auction who do, and I just became one!

I recently bought a second family home in Texas, where I live for half the year, and I bought it at auction. The person who bought it originally—the first owner—lived in it for less than six months, then defaulted. When I bought it, it was still covered by the home builder's warranty and was in almost perfect condition. The walls had to be painted, but that was it. The flooring, the appliances—everything was perfect.

My family and I now have a beautiful second home that I bought for 75 percent of what it would have cost on the open market.

Reward #6: Buying at a Discount

The most obvious benefit of buying on the courthouse steps is price. It's the real reason we're taking the previously mentioned risks and doing the legwork. The backstage real estate pass lets you buy homes for as little as 50 to 60 cents on the dollar.

That discount is about more than simply buying low so you can sell high. In addition to return on investment (ROI), a discounted price offers its own list of additional benefits, including:

- **Margin of safety.** Buying at a lower price gives you breathing room. You have a "moat" in case prices drop, the property has unexpected problems, or you have to evict a resident.
- **Easier resale.** Buying a house at 40 percent off means you're not locked into a high sale price to get your money back. If the market changes, you can afford to sell at a lower price. If your situation changes, you're not stuck with something you can't get your money out of. Paying top dollar can lead to a cascade of problems, such as overspending on renovations to try to increase the sale price. Buying at a discount gives you our second favorite benefit after profit: *options*.
- **Rent flexibility.** You don't have to sell what you buy. You can choose to rent—and sometimes an occupied property may already have the perfect tenants. Buying at a lower price gives you breathing room in your search for tenants, and it allows you some flexibility if the rental market tightens and you need to lower the rent to find tenants.

Buying at auction is the ultimate hedge. It's the best way we know to consistently buy real estate at a discount, which not only increases your returns but also gives you much more security in your business.

The Risk-Reward Connection

There are two key things you need to keep in mind about the risks and rewards of buying foreclosed homes at auction. Remember them, and your odds of success will skyrocket.

First of all, *the risks create the rewards.* If it was simple, easy, and risk-free to buy properties on the courthouse steps, everyone would do it and there would be no deals. It's as simple as that. That's why you learn to fall in love with some of the problems of buying at auction. Each risk, each potential problem, is what keeps away the people who aren't willing to do the work. It's what keeps prices lower than they are elsewhere. It is, without question, what allows you to profit.

Second, *risks can be managed.* That's the objective of our five-step process, which we outline in the next part of the book. We manage risks by coming up with a price that reflects the unknowns of buying at auction. If your research suggests problems in any of the areas above, the amount you're willing to pay will be lower.

> **LESSON:** Risks create rewards. Your goal is to price risks into the valuation of the property so that you can come up with an amount you're willing to pay for the property that allows you to earn a profit.

That's what the bulk of this book is about: learning to put together the tools, the people, the information, and the reliable process in a way that lets you manage risk. The more you stick to the process, the lower your risk will be.

CHAPTER 2
TOOLS OF THE TRADE
Outfitting Yourself as a Courthouse Warrior

The five-step process that makes up the core of this book is what has, more than anything, allowed us to consistently make money by buying foreclosures at auction. Just as important, it's also what has kept us from *losing* money.

Here's a bird's-eye view of the five steps:

- **Step 1: The List.** It's hard to buy properties at auction if you don't know they exist. Your first step is to either create or purchase a list of foreclosed properties for the area you're interested in. This list will form the backbone of your whole approach. In this step, you'll learn how to create your list and how to add to it, filter it, and analyze it to find the properties that work best for you.
- **Step 2: The Drive-By.** A picture may be worth a thousand words, but nothing is worth more than actually seeing the properties you plan to bid on. Once you've identified properties of interest, it's time to physically visit them. There are *many* tricks and techniques for gathering information on properties when you visit them—you'll learn them all.
- **Step 3: Property Analysis.** Once you've narrowed down your list to a smaller set of properties that meet your broad criteria, it's time to analyze each one to decide whether the property meets your requirements for factors such as cash flow and ROI. The goal of this analysis is to determine an upper limit for what you feel you can bid at auction.

- **Step 4: Title Review.** Once you've narrowed down your list to a few attractive deals you want to bid on, the last step before going to auction is to research the property title. Is the property the right one? Are the taxes paid? Are there other debts? Are there lien issues? This is the last stage of due diligence to make sure that the property you buy at auction can truly be transferred, free and clear, to you.
- **Step 5: The Auction.** After all the careful preparation, the most exciting moment arrives: auction day. Nothing is more thrilling—and potentially more nerve-racking—than competing on the courthouse steps with other investors. This is when all your hard work can pay off, but the auction is also a minefield for anyone new to the game. Step 5 is about mastering the very practical logistics of a typical auction day—from your arrival on-site to bidding and payment, and everything in between.

Plan the work, and work the plan. That's how you mitigate the risks of buying at auction and earn the rewards.

When we started, however, we didn't have a plan. We were just blindly stumbling forward, figuring it out as we went along. Fortunately, it worked.

At least, it worked *at first*.

After the skateboard-infused uncertainty of our first auction, we turned a nice profit on the property and immediately set our sights on doing it again. For the next few weeks we did our homework and turned up at as many auctions as we could manage, intent on finding another great deal.

We couldn't seem to repeat our success.

Auction after auction, week after week, we didn't buy a single house. We'd show up at the courthouse prepared to bid, but our property would be delayed or saved from foreclosure by a last-minute arrangement, or we would be outbid by someone else.

As the weeks passed, our first successful buy was beginning to look more and more like beginner's luck.

That was when we learned one of the most important rules of buying at auction.

Deacon versus Jasmine: Two Approaches to the Courthouse Steps

We didn't realize at the time just how lucky we were with our first property. We'd stumbled across a single home going to auction, then managed to buy it with little competition. In hindsight, that was extremely lucky—and unrepeatable.

In the years since, we've bought thousands of distressed properties, but we never relied on luck again. Instead, we've learned to look at the entire process differently.

To understand our new approach, let's compare two would-be auction buyers: Deacon and Jasmine.

Neither one has bought a foreclosure on the courthouse steps, but they're intrigued by the idea. They love real estate as a way to build wealth, and they see auctions as a more effective way to do it. They're aware that because of the lower prices, auctions offer a bigger safety moat and more potential profits. They also know that the five-step process will help them be deliberate and make smart decisions.

Although they're both excited, Deacon jumps in first. He searches out a handful of auction listings and spots a property in a neighborhood not far off. He drives by on his way to work the next morning to get a closer look.

Deacon already has a good sense of the rental market, and he has a good feeling about the place. That night, he runs the numbers, estimating the costs of renovating and running the house and calculating his maximum bid.

A title search confirms that things look promising, and as the sale date approaches, Deacon makes financial arrangements. He lines up his cashier's checks, and a few days later he heads to the auction. He arrives early, excited to start bidding.

The excitement doesn't last long.

Within a few minutes, he discovers that the place he was interested in won't be auctioned off. It was saved from foreclosure by a short sale.

The trustee conducting the auction is offering other properties, and while Deacon recognizes several, he has no real idea what they might be worth and isn't prepared to bid. Instead, he watches from the sidelines as the places are snapped up at what seem like bargain prices.

Deacon goes home discouraged. That was his first auction.

It was also his last.

Jasmine takes a different approach. She buys a list of more than *a hundred* foreclosure properties in her area. She's done her homework, and she knows that not all those properties will even make it to auction. And of those that do, only a few will fit her budget and other criteria.

To find prospects, she narrows down the list to places that meet her requirements. Eventually, she narrows down the list to ten properties that are a fit for her.

Jasmine is busy, so she hires a contractor friend to drive by the places she's selected to take pictures and get a closer look. Later, with some help from a real estate agent, she analyzes the properties to assess their value and determine her maximum bid. Then she arranges a title review to make sure she fully understands who owns each property and any liens against it.

Based on the first four steps of the process, she now has five potential properties that fit her requirements. It's time to go to auction.

When she arrives at the courthouse, Jasmine runs up against the same barrier as Deacon: Her lead pick isn't even going to be sold. In a last-minute stay of execution, the owner has found financing and sorted things out with the lender.

Fortunately, Jasmine still has four more properties she's ready to bid on.

Yet another property on her list doesn't make it to auction, but that's okay. Jasmine is outbid on the next two—the prices rise above the threshold she's already decided on—but the last one is a winner.

An hour later, she is standing in front of the house she just bought, giddy with excitement.

Jasmine is now a real estate investor.

Fishing versus Hunting

Jasmine's and Deacon's approaches were similar in many respects. They both followed the same steps. They looked for properties that fit their requirements and budget. They did their due diligence. They carefully prepared for auction.

The difference between them is that Jasmine pursued multiple options, while Deacon focused on only one. We call what Deacon was doing *hunting*. Jasmine, on the other hand, was *fishing*.

Fishing is a numbers game. You're stalking not one specific target but many. If you spend all your time trying to catch one very specific fish, you're going to spend a lot of time being disappointed.

Deacon, unfortunately, was hunting. He focused on just one property. He had, in other words, just one line in the water, hoping to find just one specific fish. That was a recipe for going home empty-handed.

Jasmine, on the other hand, understood that buying at auction is first and foremost a *numbers game*. Not numbers as in the financials of the property, but numbers as in options: You need to consider as many properties as possible to swing the odds in your favor. Jasmine knows you can't rely on catching one specific fish. You need to be strategic. You need a process. And you need to get as many lines in the water as possible.

The only way for Deacon to be successful was to get lucky. Jasmine knew that if she considered enough properties, she wouldn't need luck. Because she treated the auction as a numbers game, it was only a matter of time before Jasmine found success.

Had Deacon selected more properties to analyze, he might have found more that were a fit. Instead, he went fishing once, tried to catch a single specific fish, failed, and decided *fishing isn't for me.*

Deacon was out of the auction game before he'd even started.

> **LESSON:** Success on the courthouse steps is a numbers game. You need to find and analyze as many properties as possible.

Improving Your Numbers

Anything that increases the number of properties you can analyze is worth considering.

To play the numbers game, Jasmine did two specific things differently from Deacon. They may seem like small things—almost inconsequential—but they multiplied her odds of success enormously.

The first is that Jasmine used a simple tool—a foreclosure list—to increase the number of properties she had to choose from. While Deacon had just a few potential properties to consider, Jasmine had a hundred.

Second, Jasmine recruited other people to help. She knew she didn't have time to drive by all the properties on her first shortlist, but to ignore them would be to ignore the rule of numbers—so she hired someone to do the driving. That let her consider five times as many properties.

Great tools and great people: They're the two most effective ways to play the numbers game of buying on the courthouse steps. The first, *tools*, is covered in this chapter. The second, your *team*, is covered in the next.

> **Note:** Tools and techniques change, and we're always expanding our approach. We highly recommend you sign up for free access to our on-line resource center at **BiggerPockets.com/ForeclosureBonus**. You'll find sample spreadsheets, updated links to the best tools, checklists, and more.

The Tools of the Courthouse Warrior

The County Clerk Recorder

There are two broad ways of finding foreclosure listings. The first approach is to create a list yourself by actually looking for foreclosure notices and building your own collection of properties.

You'll find those notices at the county clerk recorder's office. Every home that is scheduled for foreclosure must have a notice filed on it. That's a legal document that is recorded by the county in which the house is located. Many counties have digitized this process and have websites where you can find properties listed for foreclosure. We'll look at this in more detail in Part II, but for now, you can find the county clerk for your area simply by searching online.

Tax Office

A search of the county clerk records can help you find properties that have notices of foreclosure associated with them. But that doesn't mean you'll know the actual address—you may have a legal property description but not a street or house number. For that, you'll need the county tax records, which are also usually kept by the county clerk. For many counties, they're readily available online. For others, you'll have to go into the county clerk's office in person.

List-Purchase Companies

If you don't want to do the legwork of digging up foreclosure listings at the county clerk's office, there are services that will do it for you. This was how Jasmine found her list.

These services generally charge a fee, but the time savings can be significant—it's a key way to expand your numbers.

When assessing list-purchase companies, note that there is often a trade-off between wide coverage and deep coverage. While a large national service might have some information everywhere, a state-level company may offer much more depth and accuracy for a particular area.

This is a fast-changing area in the foreclosure space. For the most up-to-date sources and information on how to find complete lists online, visit our resource site at BiggerPockets.com/ForeclosureBonus.

Trustee Websites

When a bank begins the foreclosure process, it hands the job of auctioning the property to a *trustee*. They're the third party who handles the foreclosure, and you'll see them on the actual courthouse steps, handling the auction itself.

Many trustees list their properties online, and finding your local foreclosure trustees is a great way to source leads.

One of the largest national players in this space is Auction.com. Not only can you find a large number of listings on their site, but they also provide an enormous amount of data on those properties, all for free. They're worth looking into. Just remember: The easier it is for you to get the information, the easier it is for everyone else, too. Don't ignore them, but don't limit your fishing to just the obvious schools.

Gmail

Whether you buy access to a list or build your own, you're going to need a place to track all the information you gather.

When you first start looking at foreclosures, you're going to be convinced that you can remember the details—the things you see on a drive-by or the information you pick up online.

You can't. After three houses, you're going to start mixing things up. You need a simple, free, and repeatable way to track your listing information, photos, neighborhood data, and property values.

Fortunately, Google has you covered. With a Gmail address, you get not only free email but also a powerful "filing cabinet" with unlimited space. In the list-building chapter, we'll show you a simple, effortless way to have Google automatically file and store your property information—including photos—so that you can find it anytime in the future with just a few keystrokes. If you don't have a Gmail address yet, get one at www.gmail.com.

Google Sheets

The best way to track and filter your prospective properties is by using a spreadsheet. You may be familiar with spreadsheet software like Microsoft Excel, but we found early on that Google's version, Sheets, gave us several advantages: It's free, and it's hosted in the cloud, which means automatic backups and access from anywhere. It's also shareable, so if you have partners, contractors, or employees, everyone can see and edit the information on your list.

If you have a Gmail address, it means you have a Google account and can access Google Sheets. With Sheets, you can create, track, and search your entire database of listing information easily and for free.

Property Data

Real estate professionals used to be the gatekeepers to almost all property data. That has changed dramatically over the past two decades.

There are now many websites that will give you much of what you'd find in a typical MLS listing—things like square footage, lot sizes, heating/cooling sources, and the like. What they also offer that MLS listings may not is more context and analysis—things like school locations and quality, price and sales history, and value estimates. Here are some of the bigger players:

- Realtor.com
- Zillow.com
- Redfin.com
- Trulia.com
- Homes.com

In theory, local MLS data is being fed to Realtor.com first, putting it a little farther upstream from the others. You may find it to be the most current and complete resource, so it may often be the first stop on your journey. Each site offers a slightly different interface and options. Over time, you'll develop an approach for analyzing properties that suits you best.

The main real estate giants, like Zillow, will also provide community and neighborhood information. Again, each varies slightly. Most people find a favorite go-to source where they start their research, and then they use others to fill the holes. For a complete list of our favorites, visit BiggerPockets.com/ForeclosureBonus.

Price/Valuation
We cover this in detail in the next chapter, but briefly, at some point, you may find that a licensed Realtor is a good source of information, particularly when it comes to estimating value. A Realtor will have access to more data than you can typically find online. More than anything, however, an experienced Realtor will often just *know*. They may have sold the same home before or seen several like it. They can also access historical sales data.

You can, however, pay for the same level of data access your local Realtor has. We offer a subscription service called Padhawk.com that offers just that.

Google Maps
You may be accustomed to using Google Maps for driving directions, but it has a number of other uses for our process. The most obvious is to locate a property, but Maps may also tell you what neighborhood the home is in, and in most cases, you'll be able to use Street View to see the actual house itself.

Interestingly, Maps will occasionally reveal property boundaries that might not be obvious in other documents. I recently analyzed a property and discovered through Maps that there was an existing severance—I was actually looking at a house and *two* lots, not just one. That immediately changed the amount we were willing to bid.

BatchGeo
While Google Maps does an exceptional job of letting you *see* a property and its surroundings, it's difficult to look at more than one property at a time. Enter BatchGeo. You can copy and paste an entire *list* of property addresses, and BatchGeo will plot them all on a map at the same time. When you're ready to drive by properties to inspect them more closely, BatchGeo can save you hours of driving by letting you see every property's location at once so you can plan your trips more efficiently.

The tools above will form the backbone of your property research. Many, if not most, are free. If you have a Gmail address and a smartphone with a data plan, you've got almost everything you need to kick off your journey to the courthouse. In later chapters, we'll go into deeper detail on how to use these simple tools to create a powerful database of potential foreclosure properties and collect enough information on them to make informed choices about whether and how much to bid.

Taking the Numbers Game to the Next Level

Remember Jasmine, our successful first-time auction buyer? Using the proper tools to be thorough in her property search gave her an edge on auction day.

But what really made the difference was the critical decision Jasmine made early on to include *other people* in her mission. While Deacon tried to do everything himself, Jasmine began to build a team.

That, as you'll see, can make all the difference.

CHAPTER 3
ASSEMBLING YOUR TEAM

How to Win at Auction by Leveraging the Power of Others

First things first: *It's possible to buy homes at auction all on your own.*

I know people who buy foreclosures and do everything themselves. They search out the notices and dig into the tax records. They drive by the homes and talk to the neighbors. They pull real estate data and crunch renovation numbers. They bid at auction.

And when they buy something? They get right in there and start swinging hammers and painting walls.

Those people have a specific set of resources and skills, and a certain mindset that makes it work. They:

- often have more surplus time than cash,
- are broadly skilled, or confident in their ability to learn on the fly,
- tend to be the DIY type, and
- approach buying at auction as a one-place-at-a-time, all-in endeavor.

In many ways, those people are the Deacons of our previous chapter.

At the other end of the spectrum are people more like Jasmine. They look at buying homes at auction as a *business*. They tend to spend money on people and services in order to increase their odds of success. They want to buy as many properties at auction as possible, provided that they can find good deals.

Those people tend to

- have more surplus cash (or *access* to cash—an important idea we'll discuss later) and less time,
- like to leverage other people's efforts, and
- surround themselves with people who already have the necessary skills and are better at using those skills.

In the previous chapter, Jasmine was taking her first fledgling steps toward becoming the second type of auction buyer. She wasn't wealthy, but she was judiciously choosing where to allocate her resources to serve her best.

When I started buying at auction, I was a lot like the first type of buyer. I would drive by all the houses myself. I'd take pictures of them and create files for each one. I'd do title research on all of them and go online to figure out what the pricing should be. Then I would put in my best guesses for rehab costs and go bid on the properties at auction. It worked, but I missed out on a lot of properties, and progress was slow in the beginning.

If you have—or think you can develop—all the skills you need and you want to do it on your own, go for it. You could even head straight to Part II and start reviewing the five steps.

But before you do, it's worth considering the bigger picture.

Most of us need a little help in life. We're not experts at *everything*. You might be great with spreadsheets but terrible with hammers, or perhaps the opposite. You might love to go to auction but not have the time to drive to every address to do the legwork beforehand. You might be short on time but have some money—or the reverse.

Whatever your situation, you're almost certainly going to need help with at least some of the tasks on the road to buying and profiting on your first auction house. That help doesn't have to cost a lot—or anything, as you'll see—but it's best to go into the process with your eyes open.

And remember: Success is about *fishing*. It's about numbers, and the best way to multiply your numbers is to get help.

Time, Money, and Teleportation

What tends to discourage people from getting help, however, is *cost*. "Every dollar I spend paying for something," such people say, "is a dollar I'm giving up."

While that may seem true, it's worth digging into.

The biggest challenge for most newcomers to the foreclosure business is indeed numbers—but not *financial* numbers. It's *property numbers*, or in other words, simply being able to identify, analyze, and bid on enough homes to be successful.

Jasmine used a purchased list to increase the total pool of foreclosures to choose from, but she also hired someone to drive by the properties she knew she didn't have time check out on her own. Likewise, if there are two auctions in your area on the same day at the same time and you pay a bidder to attend on your behalf, you aren't just trading money for time; you're trading a little money for effectively *doubling* your odds of success by being at twice as many auctions. It's as if you've developed teleportation powers so you can be in two places at once!

Auctions are all about fishing, and the more lines in the water, the better. If buying a second rod and reel and paying someone to cast it doubles your chances, that's at least worth considering.

In this chapter, we'll look at the people and skills that are most likely to increase your odds, reduce your mistakes, and lead you to a successful first bid on the courthouse steps.

> **LESSON:** Building a team is an enormous multiplier for your numbers. You're only one person. If you're serious about buying on the courthouse steps, you need to be serious about asking for help.

Your Auction A-Team

Have you ever watched a heist movie? They often start with a montage of scenes that show the team being put together. Each member has a special skill set. Without the full team, the scheme falls apart, and no one profits.

Think of this as similar: You need a diverse array of skilled people who can help you be successful. But instead of safecrackers, explosives experts, and alarm techs, you may want the following.

Property Scouts Drivers

Like Jasmine, one of the first people I hired was a property driver.

The drive-by, which we'll talk about in Step 2, is incredibly valuable. It seems simple—and it is—but I can't imagine buying homes at auction without doing drive-bys. The challenge is that they can be very time-consuming.

In the beginning, I only wanted to buy homes that were unoccupied. We didn't yet know how to evict tenants, and it seemed like another layer of risk and complication. I wanted to focus on homes that were empty, period.

The trick was that, although I might have a list of a hundred homes slated for auction, I had no idea which ones were unoccupied. The only way to make an educated guess was to visit each home in person. But visiting a hundred homes? That was days of work—days that cut into analyzing and valuing the properties and preparing for and attending auctions.

I knew that of those hundred homes, less than a quarter might be vacant or meet my other criteria (things like age, or price, which we'll get to). I reasoned that if someone else could identify those twenty-five or so places, I could drive by them myself and really dig in. I would still be driving, but it would be high-value driving.

Since those early days, the role of property scout has developed into a real job. People pay for it. People do it. It's not usually a full-time job, however, and you can generally pay people on a per-drive or per-address basis.

The criteria for choosing a driver? Look for someone who:

- can drive and has a reasonably decent-looking vehicle,
- is willing to work part-time on a per-drive or per-address basis,
- has a smartphone to upload photos and text, and
- isn't afraid to knock on doors and talk to people (this is crucial, as you'll see later).

Real Estate Professionals

Before auction day, there's one single number you need to arrive at for each house you're interested in, and that's your maximum bid—the most you're willing to pay for the property at auction. Ideally, it captures all the information you've gathered, as well as the unknowns, and turns them into a number you think makes sense.

Coming up with that number, which we'll explore later, is an area you might consider getting help with. For most people, a Realtor or other real estate professional is the logical choice. They generally have extensive experience with your market, and they have access to lots of data. Unless you have some experience and use a service like PadHawk, a Realtor will simply know more than you.

Generally, this can go one of two ways. Either you pay a fee for the Realtor to give you an opinion of the value of each listing, or the Realtor helps you out in the hopes of representing you as the listing agent in the future when you sell the homes you buy at auction. I got started by reaching out to four or five agents. One responded, helped me with valuations for free, and then went on to make a healthy return on that investment by becoming the listing agent for many properties we sold.

Title Researchers

You can do your own title research—we'll cover that in Step 4—but you can also have it done for you. There are two ways to approach outsourcing this job. The first is to simply pay a professional. There are companies that specialize in title review work. The upside is that you'll be hiring someone who knows their way around and understands the nuances of title work.

You can also hire someone who's inexperienced and teach them the job. But before you can teach anyone else, you'll need to log some experience doing it yourself first.

Don't pick the muddy middle ground of paying someone who is inexperienced if *you* don't have experience either. Title is worth taking seriously.

Auction Bidders

The actual auction might seem like the least likely part of the process to outsource, but there are reasons why you might want to have someone else represent you at auction to do the bidding.

The most compelling is that in some areas, multiple auctions happen on the same day in different locations—and they all may have properties you're interested in. You can't be in two places at once.

The same is true of the auction itself. There are often multiple trustees selling at the same place on the same day. Trying to bid on more than one place at the same time is very challenging. It can also be overwhelming at first; some people choose to have a professional bidder represent them initially while they adjust to the chaos of several hundred properties being sold by multiple trustees in a short time.

Auctions are not always comfortable affairs, either. They tend to be held outside, and the weather doesn't usually change that. Homes are sold rain or shine, in the heat or cold, and standing around for a few hours on a lousy day requires a certain temperament.

In short: You may get your best results at auction if you have someone else you can lean on.

The person you choose to represent you at auction will not only need to be available on specific auction dates (no flexibility there) but they'll have to be reliable—after all, they'll be walking around with your cashier's checks in their pocket.

As a rule, you'll pay more for an auction bidder than you would for a property scout, but if hiring one makes the difference between closing a great deal or missing out, you'll find it's money well spent.

Attorneys

I didn't use an attorney for the first fifteen or twenty houses I bought at auction. Normally when you buy a home, lawyers are involved to make sure the money changes hands properly, register title changes and mortgages, and take care of the legal minutiae. When you buy a property at auction, those tasks are generally performed by you and by the trustee running the auction.

When you start buying houses that are occupied, however, you'll likely want a lawyer who specializes in evictions. Regardless, use an attorney or a firm that specializes in real estate law. That way, if you run into complications or need legal help with any other part of the process, you'll have an expert to turn to.

Locksmiths

One of your first jobs after purchase is to change the locks. This is always good policy, and not something you want to try to save a few dollars on or leave until later. Locksmiths are easy to find. Use one.

Tradespeople and Contractors

It's wise to assume that any home you buy at auction is going to need some work. The property might need anything from a quick cleaning to a considerable renovation, but it's going to need *something*.

Painters and cleaners are the most likely pros you'll need. Even a well-cared-for home will have to be painted after the owners move out. At some point you're going to need plumbers, carpenters, and electricians, as well.

Bankers, Lenders, and Financial Partners

When it comes to the courthouse steps, cash is generally king. In most cases, you'll need to pay immediately—or within a very narrow time frame—for what you buy.

It's difficult to get traditional mortgages for auction properties because appraisers and inspectors can't get inside the homes to see them.

We'll discuss this in detail in a later chapter. For now, just remember this: *If you can find great deals, great money will follow.* While *you* might not have the money to bid on certain properties, someone else does. A financial partner might be just what you need.

Tips for Building a Great Team

For many people, getting help is a barrier. Here are a few extra lessons we've learned along the way that might smooth the road ahead.

You're Not Hiring Full-Time

It's important to remember that you're almost certainly not hiring anyone full-time—at least, not at first. You probably don't need the burden of a payroll right off the bat. Instead, you want to look at the work that has to be done and decide on the best way to make it happen. That choice is different for everyone.

Think of your team first and foremost as a trusted network that you build over time and can turn to for the things you need.

It Takes Time to Find Greatness

One of the most common mistakes people make is to give up looking for good help after one bad experience. It takes time to find great people, but *it's worth the investment.* There's nothing more reassuring or satisfying than being able to send one message to someone and know that the job you need to get done will be done, and done well.

For example, if you don't find the right driver right away, try again. Don't be discouraged if the first one doesn't work out. It doesn't cost much to see how someone performs by giving them a single task. And don't settle for anyone who isn't great—at least not for long.

One Person Can Fill Many Roles

The search for the right person can pay off in other ways, too. I've had

Realtors analyze properties, then represent me at auction, and then list the house for sale after we purchase it. As you'll see in the next section, *any* part of the auction process can be learned, and it can also be taught. If you find the right person, keep using them and consider using them for a wider range of tasks.

Work by Referral

When you find a great person, keep them. Better yet, ask *them* for more great people. This can work particularly well with contractors—get referrals from someone who is terrific at what they do and *tell* them that you were referred by so-and-so. Quality is contagious, and great tradespeople like to work with other great tradespeople.

Fishing and the Love of the Process

Have you ever noticed just how much fishermen love to fish? They'll get up in the dark, head out in the cold and the rain, freeze for hours, catch nothing—and then get up and do it again the next day. At times, it seems they don't even care whether they catch anything.

Fishermen love their sport because they truly love *fishing* more than *catching*. They're process-driven. All that boating around, testing baits, and analyzing currents, temperature, and profiles of the fish "neighborhood" is part of the great joy of the game. Fishermen like it more when they catch, but they keep fishing even if they don't because they love the act of fishing itself.

Buying at auction is similar. You need to fall in love with the process. You need to enjoy digging up information on properties, filtering lists to find the right properties for you, investigating those you think are promising, and crunching numbers.

Like fishermen, successful auction buyers are process-driven. We break our process into five distinct steps. We don't skimp, and we don't skip. Every step has a purpose, and they all depend on each other. Following the process is the most important thing you can do.

Here's why:

- It focuses on finding properties that suit *you*—your risk tolerance, your budget, your skills.
- It reduces risk. The process is designed to reduce or eliminate the biggest risks of auction—those we discussed in Chapter 1.

- It protects you from yourself. It's easy to get swept up in the excitement of a specific home, or the potential for huge profits, or the exhilaration of an auction. The process helps you stay grounded and rational. When it comes to buying foreclosures at auction, being grounded and rational is essential.
- It delivers the best returns. Financial gain isn't the only reason to follow the process, but it's a big one. The process helps you narrow down your search to properties that make financial sense. Otherwise, buying foreclosed properties at auction is not worth your time and effort.

As they say: *Plan the work and work the plan.* That's how you find great properties, how you buy them at the best price, and how you turn that price into profits.

Wait! There Are Resources!

Hey! We're about to launch into Part II, which details the five steps of our process. It's the nitty-gritty of how to find, analyze, and bid on foreclosures at auction.

We've put together a great resource page to go with this section. It has checklists, spreadsheets, calculators, links, maps, and all kinds of other goodies, all of which will make your life a lot easier.

Note: You can find everything at **BiggerPockets.com/ForeclosureBonus**.

BIDDING TO BUY

PART II
THE FIVE STEPS

CHAPTER 4
STEP 1:
THE LIST
Finding Your Ideal Foreclosures

Remember Deacon and Jasmine, our fictional first-time auction attendees?

Of the two, Jasmine had the most success at auction. She understood the numbers game of foreclosures and played it well, using tools and people to increase the number of potential properties she could consider. Deacon, on the other hand, picked only one property, which never even made it to the courthouse steps.

Our experience in the weeks that followed our first purchase was closer to Deacon's. We attended auction after auction but couldn't seem to buy anything. We struggled to duplicate our original success, but each week we went home empty-handed.

The biggest barrier for us, it turned out, was the same one Deacon faced: The homes we were interested in simply weren't appearing at auction like they were supposed to. We would show up at the courthouse ready to bid, but the properties we wanted would be mysteriously absent.

Over time, we discovered that only about 20 percent of properties scheduled for sale on a given date would actually be auctioned that day. Gradually, we began to understand that foreclosures could be delayed or canceled for a host of reasons, including:

- The homeowner paid the outstanding amount.

- The bank decided to give the homeowner more time, either to pay up or to sell the home.
- The owner filed for bankruptcy.
- The owner filed a lawsuit to slow or cancel the foreclosure.
- The home sold before the auction.

As we gained experience, we learned that the challenge didn't end there. Of the 20 percent or so of listings that actually went to auction, perhaps only 50 percent were a good deal.

When you put those two stats together, the need for using a fishing approach becomes very apparent. If you want to *buy* at auction, not just watch, you need to start with as many potential properties as possible. As soon as we began increasing the number of homes we analyzed and the number of auctions we attended, we began to find repeatable success in foreclosures.

That brings us to the first of our five steps to a successful day at the courthouse: *to create a complete list of multiple properties slated for foreclosure instead of focusing on a single property.*

It's Worth It

Before we begin, however, consider one more thing.

You might find the statistics above discouraging. After all, for each property you consider, you are, in effect, becoming a kind of private investigator, digging up information and clues that can help you determine a fit and a price. All that detective work takes time, so why go through the trouble of creating a list when so many properties either won't be a fit or won't appear at auction? Why not just purchase a list of houses slated for auction, and skip all the Sherlock Holmes business?

There are three good reasons.

The first is simply that **there's no better teacher than experience**. You'll gain a world of in-depth knowledge of the industry, the market, and the foreclosure process by doing the legwork yourself. Even if you decide to purchase a list, running through the process in this chapter just a couple of times will be well worth the effort.

The second reason to take the DIY approach is that, **even if a property doesn't go to auction on the originally scheduled date, it might reappear in the future**. Most of the reasons that houses don't go to auction are about *delay*, not deletion. Homeowners may declare bankruptcy, but that just slows the process. They may convince the bank to give them more time, but that doesn't mean they'll be able to catch up on their payments. A home might sell before auction only to have the sale fall through at closing. We've seen properties postponed at auction a half-dozen times before finally selling months later. That means the work you do to build a list now can pay off months, or even years, down the road.

The last, and arguably the most important, reason for trying out list-building yourself, is that it speaks to one of the main themes of this book: **Going the extra mile to do what others won't gives you an edge on auction day.** When you build a list yourself, you see the source documents—the real data. You know what information is available. By going through the DIY process, you'll be better able to judge the quality of a list for sale. Moreover, in some states and counties, the data in list services is far from complete. Better still, in some areas, *no one* is doing the research necessary to put those listings online or make them available for purchase.

The process of building your own list is more than just an opportunity to educate yourself; in some cases, it's an opportunity to be the only one with the information—and that's the best advantage of all.

> **LESSON:** Experience is the best teacher and a competitive advantage. Even if you eventually decide to outsource the steps of the process, you'll learn an enormous amount by trying them yourself first.

Before you begin: Visit the resource page!

1. The easiest way to start compiling your list of foreclosure notices is to use a spreadsheet. You can download a free spreadsheet from our foreclosure resource page at BiggerPockets.com/ForeclosureBonus.
2. Every county is different. To get a real feel for what searching for foreclosures online is like, we've made a short video to walk you through the process—it's available on the resource page as well.
3. Naturally, you don't *have* to build your own list. You can buy a list too. The resource site also has information on list vendors.

How to Build Your First Foreclosure List

1. Find the County Clerk's Office Online

Lenders can't just show up and take a house without following due process. Every home that is scheduled for foreclosure needs to have a legal notice filed on it, and that notice is recorded at the county clerk's office. Some states may call this official a *county recorder* or a *recorder of deeds*, but regardless of what the official is called, their office is your first stop in creating your list.

Simply search for your county with the term "recorder" and you should find what you need. We'll use Sacramento County as an example.

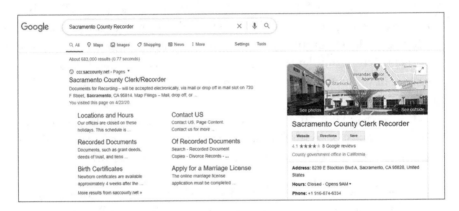

2. Search for Notices

Once you find your county recorder online, it's time to start looking for actual foreclosure notices.

Not every state posts these notices online, although it's becoming increasingly common. If they are not available online, they are available in person at the recorder's office. That's how it still works where we started, in Sacramento County. You can search for notices online, but you have to view the actual documents in person. You'll see reference to a "document search" or a "records search" or something similar. Each county's website is different. Some offer a free and easy search interface, complete with maps and property information, while others charge a fee. Some are cumbersome and slow. Other counties have almost nothing online, and the only way to get information is to actually go into the office yourself and request it in person.

The documents you're looking for are usually referred to by one of the following terms (or something similar):

- Notice of sale
- Notice of trustee sale
- Notice of foreclosure

The word "notice" may or may not appear; again, each county is different, and their websites also change regularly. If you search for "Bell County trustee sale," for example, the first search result is for a list of all foreclosure notices on the Bell County site. Not all counties make things this easy; some almost seem to go out of their way to make things as tricky as possible, but it's always worth checking first. You simply have to visit each site and start poking around.

When you find a notice, you should be able to click on it to view the details of the foreclosure document.

If the more complicated county websites seem intimidating, don't be discouraged—after all, the easier the information is to find, the more competition you'll have on auction day. The difficult counties reward the persistent people who are willing to put in a little extra time!

Here is an example search and county website
that provides the notices for free.

Foreclosure Notices

Foreclosure Sales are held on the First Tuesday of Each Month, unless 51.002 (a-1) If the first Tuesday of a month occurs on January 1 or July 4, a public sale under Subsection (a) must be held between 10 a.m. and 4 p.m. on the first Wednesday of the month.

On June 1, 2010, the Bell County Commissioner's Court approved Minute Order #197/10 the designation, Pursuant to Texas Property Code, Section 51.002, of public sales of real property subject to contractual liens shall be held at the:

Bell County Clerk's alcove to the east of the main entrance of the Bell County Justice Complex, 1201 Huey Drive, Belton, Texas beginning August 3, 2010.

Filings:	Filling Fee:	Records Mgmt Fee (LGC 118.0216)	Courthouse Security(LGC 291.008)	Total
Foreclosure Posting by Trustee/Attorney - Property Code 51.002	$2.00		$1.00	$3.00
Foreclosure Posting by County Clerk - Property Code 51.002, LGC 118.011(c)	$12.00		$1.00	$13.00

May	June
May Foreclosure Notices (1)	June Foreclosure Notices (1)
May Foreclosure Notices (2)	June Foreclosure Notices (2)
May Foreclosure Notices (3)	June Foreclosure Notices (3)
May Foreclosure Notices (4)	June Foreclosure Notices (4)
May Foreclosure Notices (5)	
May Foreclosure Notices (6)	

3. Capture the Foreclosure Notice Data

The notice of sale documents you find will contain a range of information, much of which is going to be useful. The key is to start capturing that data so you can sort and analyze it later.

Here's some of the information you *may* find in a foreclosure notice:

- Legal description of the property
- Property address
- Lender's name
- Loan document name/number
- Scheduled sale (auction) date

Create a spreadsheet, and add anything relevant to it. Again, your best option here is to start with our template at BiggerPockets.com/ForeclosureBonus. It's free and it will save you time and ensure you capture all the information you'll need.

Remember: What you're looking at is just a foreclosure notice. It's a legal document that tells us that a property is scheduled to be sold at auction, but it doesn't have everything we need. In fact, sometimes it won't even have a complete property address. For that, and more, we have to to move on.

Example Notice of Trustee Sale

Here is the start of the spreadsheet:

Owner	Lender	Loan Date	Doc #	Legal	County	Auction Time	Sale Date	Trustee
Antonette L Parnell	Wells Fargo	2/24/11	2011-00006961	Lot 2, Blk 3, Stagecoach Rd	Bell	10:00 AM	5/5/20	Angela Zavala

4. Find and Search the County Tax Records

Unlike the previously mentioned foreclosure notices, county tax records are complete when it comes to property address and owner information. That information is public, and most counties make it available online.

Your next job, then, is to find the tax record for any property you've identified in the previous step, usually beginning by searching for the property owner name and/or whatever address information you have.

The tax records can provide some critical information you may not find elsewhere, such as:

- Complete street address and legal description
- Property tax status, including any outstanding taxes
- Year of construction
- Assessment information, such as assessed/market value
- Square footage and number/type of rooms

You won't necessarily find all those items, but each bit of information helps. Add it all to your spreadsheet.

Property Details	
Account	
Property ID:	44467
Legal Description:	STAGECOACH ROAD PHASE I, BLOCK 003, LOT 0002
Geographic ID:	0425465083
Agent Code:	
Type:	Real
Location	
Address:	705 SPOKE DR KILLEEN, TX
Map ID:	41806-B24
Neighborhood CD:	STGCHRDPH1
Owner	
Owner ID:	735262
Name:	PARNELL, ANTONETTE L
Mailing Address:	705 SPOKE DR KILLEEN, TX 76542-9022
% Ownership:	100.0%
Exemptions:	For privacy reasons not all exemptions are shown online

Property Values	
Improvement Homesite Value:	$68,104
Improvement Non-Homesite Value:	$0
Land Homesite Value:	$7,200
Land Non-Homesite Value:	$0
Agricultural Market Valuation:	$0
Market Value:	$75,304
Ag Use Value:	$0
Appraised Value:	$75,304
Homestead Cap Loss: ❓	$0
Assessed Value:	$75,304

DISCLAIMER Information provided for research purposes only. Legal descriptions and acreage amounts are for appraisal district use only and should be verified prior to using for legal purpose and or documents. Please contact the Appraisal District to verify all information for accuracy.

We found the address, year built, and assessed value:

Address	Year Built	Assessed Value	Owner
705 Spoke Dr, Killeen TX	1977	$75,304	Antonette L Parnell

5. Search Real Estate Data Sources

Once you've finished with the county tax records, it's time to move out of the realm of local government sources and into the wide-open spaces of online real estate data.

There are numerous online sources for property data, and they change constantly. (See our resource page for links.) You'll find that some sites work better for some counties. Maybe Redfin is a great choice for the county you're working in, while in another county, Zillow may be best.

You can type any address into these sites and find an abundance of extra information for your growing database, including:
- Estimated value
- Estimated rent
- Square footage, number of bedrooms, number of bathrooms, etc.
- Construction date
- Neighborhood data, such as schools, local amenities
- Interior and exterior photos
- Mechanical and HVAC info
- Price and tax history

Much of this will be beyond what you found at the county clerk's office, and worth adding to your spreadsheet.

At this point, it's also a good idea to pull up a Google Map of each property. You'll be able to see the surrounding area, and sometimes even see lot divisions to identify property boundaries. Use the "share" feature in Google Maps to copy a link to the map. Paste that link into your spreadsheet too—you'll need it for further analysis later, and having the link will save you from searching for the property each time you want to see it.

Now we have all the property details we will need. Keep adding to the spreadsheet:

Address	Bed	Bath	SF	Zestimate	Rent Zesti-mate	Year Built	Zillow URL	Google URL
705 Spoke Dr, Killeen TX	3	1.5	1456	$103,075	$1,075	1977	https://www.	https://www.

Filtering Your List

Complete the above steps for all the properties in the county that you found trustee sale notices for. Once you've done that, you'll have a list of properties in the form of a spreadsheet where each row contains data on a home scheduled to be sold at auction.

While all these homes are scheduled for foreclosure, they are *not* all of equal interest to you. We're following our fishing rule of simply trying to keep a lot of lines in the water because we know that improves our odds of making a great catch. But, as with fishing, sometimes you catch fish you aren't interested in. Now it's time to throw back all the fish that are too small, too big, too old, etc.

We call this *filtering the list*. We're taking the larger list we've compiled and tossing out everything that doesn't fit our criteria.

This filtering process is critical because it (a) allows you to apply your future efforts to a smaller number of houses, so you don't waste your time and money, and (b) helps you identify the homes that *fit*—those that meet your budget and other criteria. Filtering is your first step toward profitability. When you narrow your list down to just homes that fit, you're vastly improving your odds of being successful.

In the chapters ahead, you'll be culling your list a little further, shrinking the list of *possibles* down to *ideals* and putting a price on those you want to bid on. But there are a few filters you can apply right away to shrink your current catch down to fish that look like they might really be worth keeping.

If you've built your spreadsheet correctly or used our template, you can sort your listings by any of the following criteria.

Price

For most people, this is the very first sorting criterion. There's no point in continuing with the rest of the steps in the process for a house that isn't within your budget.

You won't always know in advance what the minimum, if any, bid on a property will be. However, if you've done your homework, you'll know one significant piece of information: the amount owed on the mortgage. Since foreclosure is an effort to recoup an outstanding debt, it's a reasonable assumption that the amount outstanding on the property is a place to begin our price sorting.

The trustees charged with auctioning off houses have restrictions on where they start the bidding. While the bidders can drive the price as high as they want, trustees in most areas can't *start* the bidding anywhere they choose—the upper limit is the amount owed, plus reasonable costs like interest accrued and attorney fees.

That means that if we know the amount of outstanding debt, we can at least make a guess as to the highest opening bid. A property with a $100,000 outstanding mortgage balance might have a minimum opening bid as low as zero (trustees can go as *low* as the lender will allow) or as high as $120,000, but likely not more.

If you have a $100,000 auction budget, you're probably not going to bother digging any further on a property with a $200,000 mortgage. It's just not worth the extra legwork.

A good rule of thumb? Start with properties with outstanding mortgage balances that are close to or less than your available funds.

Age

Age is an easy search criterion, and most people use it simply to reduce the potential unknowns of getting a place ready to rent or sell.

If you have the interest or skills to do more significant renovations and upgrades, you might look at homes built more than twenty years ago. If you're looking for a good deal on a low-maintenance rental, a newer home is best for you.

Location/Neighborhood

For many people, location is another easy sort. You might choose:

- Counties close to where you live
- Specific areas where you have some knowledge of the market and values
- Communities with certain amenities or that lack HOA restrictions
- Areas that have properties that are more likely to fall within your price range

Remember, that sorting is just a tool. You're not committing to buying a property that stays on your list. What you *are* doing is saying, "I'm willing to put some more time into this one. I think it's worth it."

The following is an example of a list of 90 homes that was filtered to just those built after 2009, after which there are only 12 homes left. Remember you can use any of the concepts above to filter to houses that will fit your strategy.

Address	SF	Assessed Value	Year Built	Owner
705 Spoke Dr, Killeen TX	1456	$75,304	1977	Antonette L Parnell
3302 LORNE DR	3196	256063	2017	SMITH
5902 TAFFINDER LN	2705	217621	2017	QUICHOCHO
0 FM 2115	4800	379933	2016	GRANILLO
4910 PREWITT RANCH RD	2633	224406	2015	COTE
1359 HOMESTEAD	2059	207973	2014	CAMACHO
6407 CREEK LAND RD	3629	265606	2013	DE MAYO
2609 GREEN GIANT DR	2443	291508	2012	JOSEPH
3400 CASTLETON DR	2485	198327	2012	WALKER
422 SLAWSON LN	1872	54778	2012	CHILDERS
3302 CRICKLEWOOD DR	3541	252130	2011	FOSTER
5803 TURQUOISE DR	1685	184084	2011	HARLEE
7008 ANDALUCIA ST	2140	229457	2010	JAHR

Note: Should You Invest Out of State?

Budget is often a primary constraint for new buyers, and many consider going farther afield to find properties they can afford. However, there is a trade-off involved. Homes that are closer to you are easier for you to drive by and analyze. If you decide to shop outside your area, make sure you budget for the extra time and expense that will entail.

Listin' Ain't Easy

Keep in mind that this process gets *much* easier with experience. It may seem time-consuming initially, but you'll get better as you become familiar with the listings. Most buyers, especially at first, buy close to home or in a county they're familiar with. As a result, they quickly become comfortable with each county's particular way of doing things. They learn the lingo, where to click, and how to get the most information in the shortest possible time.

When you see twenty or thirty different versions of trustee sales receipts and property records, you learn your way around the world of foreclosures quickly.

What about the houses that stump you? Don't be afraid to simply let go of a difficult property. Not all properties are created equal. Some demand more time than others. It may be in your best interest to simply skip a property that's more complex than others. Remember, you don't have to buy every property, and you certainly don't have to analyze every single one either.

When you've finished filtering your list, you should have a shorter list of properties that are a fit for your interests, skills, and budget. Each one should be a house that you're willing to commit to the next step in the process: the drive-by.

Note: For sample notices, spreadsheet templates, and more, visit **BiggerPockets.com/ForeclosureBonus.**

CHAPTER 5
STEP 2: THE DRIVE-BY

Mastering the Most Important Tool in Your Courthouse Toolbox

A few years ago, I saw a promising property on an auction list for the northern Sacramento area. It was in a high-end neighborhood not far from where I lived, so I drove over to see the house myself.

First impressions were encouraging. The nearby homes were a half-million dollars and up, set back from clean streets, and expensively landscaped. I knew that if we could get a great deal on a place in this area, we'd be able to flip the house easily.

I pulled up to the address on the listing to find that the home itself looked as good as those on the rest of the block: manicured lawn, perfect landscaping, and a squeaky-clean exterior.

At that point, the easy approach would have been to verify the address, take some pictures, and drive away. After all, this was either an occupied and well-loved home or it was an unoccupied but extremely well-maintained home; either way, the place was probably in excellent condition inside.

But easy doesn't get you wins at auction. Instead, I hopped out of the car and strolled up the walk to knock on the door in hopes of finding someone at home.

As I got closer, something stood out against the perfect exterior. The front door, which was otherwise immaculate, had two very large dents in its steel exterior.

Now I was curious. Big dents in a door generally mean someone had to break that door in, and there are only a handful of reasons for that.

When I got no answer to my knock, I walked to the left side of the house and peeked in the window. At first, everything looked fine—to one side, I could tell the place was in excellent shape, with nice finishes. But as I peered in the other direction, the house seemed *dark*.

I thought perhaps the paint was a darker tone or the blinds were closed, but as my eyes adjusted, I could see the real story: There had been a fire in an entire wing of the house.

Start Up Your Best Risk-Management Tool

In Chapter 1 we looked at the key risks of buying homes at auction. Those risks are real, but we learned two critical things about them. The first is that the *risks create the reward*—if there were no risk to foreclosures, everyone would want them, and there'd be no profits to be found. The second critical idea is that *risks can be mitigated*. With some elbow grease and a good strategy, you can manage and reduce the exposure of buying at auction. That's the sweet spot—you get access to the rewards while keeping your risk as low as possible.

Let's review that list of risks:

1. **List Accuracy.** Is the information I'm seeing correct?
2. **Property Condition.** Can I profitably get this house ready for rent or resale?
3. **Occupancy.** Are there occupants in the house that could negatively affect my plans for the property?
4. **Clear Title.** Can I get the legal right to control the future of this property?
5. **Valuation.** Can I buy this property at an attractive price?

Because the information on foreclosed homes is imperfect, each of these areas holds some unknowns for us. The best way to manage them is through information—the more you know about a property, the better. And hands down, the single best tool in your information arsenal is your *car*.

That's right. Simply driving by a property—or having someone do it for you if you have partners or a team—is the best way to fill in those unknown blanks on your spreadsheet. A drive-by can give you critical information on four of the five key risks in buying foreclosures (we'll cover *clear title* in Step 4), and each bit of information decreases your risk and increases your odds of success.

The house I'd found looked ideal until I hopped in my car. Only the thorough drive-by process revealed that the house had actually *been on fire*. That was the single most important piece of information about the home, and no amount of online research would have revealed it. It was something that had to be seen in person.

Most homes, of course, haven't been on fire. Still, it's not an exaggeration to say that a good drive-by has more impact than any other single stage of the process. In this chapter, we're going to map out, step by step, what makes a great drive-by.

Your Drive-By Goals

Each time you visit a property, you're trying to gather information in four areas. The more you can gather, the better positioned you'll be for the next steps in our process, when each bit of information helps you decide the upper limit of what you're willing to bid at auction. The four areas are:

1. **Neighborhood.** Identical houses in very different areas can be worth very different amounts. Your first job as you enter the community where the house is located is to take note of the big picture.

2. **Address/Listing Accuracy.** An important purpose of the drive-by is simply to *make sure you're buying a house that exists*. That may sound a little dramatic, but it isn't. Mistakes happen. The drive-by is a chance to avoid them.

3. **Occupancy.** As a general rule, an unoccupied house presents fewer challenges after auction. There are no eviction delays or costs, and fewer uncertainties. This isn't always the case—the person living in the house might provide the perfect new tenant, for example. But determining whether anyone is living in the property is a key part of the drive-by process.

4. **Condition and Value.** One of the great unknowns of buying at auction is the condition and quality of the inside of a home. It's easy to get a sense of the outside condition of a home when you see it, but the inside is a mystery. Fortunately, it's one that we can use a few tricks to unravel.

Let's work through each of these in turn, starting from your first approach to the home.

The Drive-By Process

1. Scout the Neighborhood

As they say in real estate, *location, location, location*. Identical houses in different areas will have different values, and your first order of business in the drive-by begins before you even reach the house.

As you enter the community the house is located in, take note of:

- **Community/area name.** Not every community has a name, but many do. You can often see this on Google Maps, and you may find signage as you enter a community. Many online sources provide great aggregate data grouped around a community—schools, walkability, safety, average home value, etc. Knowing the community can also help you identify the year a home was built.
- **Other listings.** Are there other homes listed for sale? Those make for easy references to research online. If a home very similar to the one you're interested in is selling just down the street, you can look it up online and get not only a sense of valuation but sometimes even a glimpse into floor plans and finish quality if the neighborhood is made up of very similar models. Watch for real estate signs!
- **Relativity.** Is the home you're interested in the largest on the block? The smallest? Is it the only single-story? Often the extremes are harder to sell. Also, the home's relative size and quality compared to others gives you a reference point for valuation.

2. Verify the Address

After you visit enough homes, it's easy to become a little complacent. The navigation system on your phone says, "Your destination is the third house on the left." You pull up, you see an uncut lawn with mail stacking up on the front steps, and think *this must be it.*

Not so fast.

Following the easy route has got us into trouble. In fact, we've bought the wrong house more than once. I'm not kidding.

One time, there were two foreclosure properties listed on the same street. We heard the trustee call out the property address at auction but ended up bidding on the wrong house. Another time, we bought a house, then showed up to change the locks only to discover that we were at the wrong place! In that instance, there was a typo on the auction list. We'd scouted and analyzed the wrong property.

Double-check the address. Look for a house number. Cross-check it with your spreadsheet. Then try to ask an occupant and a neighbor. And pay attention at auction—on the auction sheet, only one word separates 123 Pine Street from 123 Pine Avenue, but in real life there's an enormous difference between the two!

3. Determine Occupancy

Even though we've bought occupied houses at auction, we prefer to buy vacant homes.

There are some upsides to a home with someone in it—the person who lives there might, for example, become a tenant. Also, occupied homes tend to better maintained. Nonetheless, in our experience, buying an empty property is simply easier and entails less overall risk.

We recently bought an occupied home only to discover that the lender had wrongly foreclosed on the borrower; the house should never have been at auction in the first place. After the deal had already gone through, the occupants filed a lawsuit for wrongful foreclosure and won. That was eighteen months ago. We're the owner of record on the deed, but we still face the complicated situation of getting the lender to cover our interest expenses and reimburse the owner for damages. Eventually, it will all work out, but in the meantime, it's a complex, money-losing arrangement, since we've had cash invested in that house the whole time.

Mind you, this isn't the norm. We've had only two similar instances out of thousands. Even when we have to go through the legal eviction process, it's usually not this complicated. If we know a home is occupied, we adjust the amount we're willing to bid accordingly. That adjustment is almost always enough to deal with any extra complications. Still, we like vacant properties best.

You might choose differently, of course, but as with house fires, you can't determine whether a home is occupied just by looking at online listings or county documents. You need to go see it for yourself.

I would estimate that we're able to correctly determine occupancy about 90 percent of the time during the drive-by process.

We do that by:

- **Looking for obvious signs.** Sometimes there are cars in the driveway or kids playing in the yard. Either is a pretty clear sign of occupancy. Other times, there are bank notices on the door, the grass is a foot tall, and the front door is ajar. Those are pretty clear signs the place is empty.
- **Knocking on the door.** Even when you see signs of occupancy, it's wise to knock and try to speak with someone. If no one answers, that doesn't tell you the place is unoccupied, but if someone does, that will usually confirm that someone lives there.
- **Talking to neighbors.** The closest neighbors can give you a wealth of information. They will almost always know whether a home is occupied. We've even had neighbors show us through vacant properties!

Often, however, the signs are a little less clear. There might be a car in the driveway, but what exactly does that mean? A closer look will reveal if the tags are current, if the car is dusty and unused, or if the tires are flat.

Other tricks include turning on the outdoor tap for the hose. If no water comes out, that may be indicate the water is shut off to the entire home—another sign of vacancy.

You'll be able to do a little more snooping at homes that are *not* occupied. For example, you can sneak a peek in the windows if you like. Just remember, you'll need to be able to justify what you're doing.

My rule of thumb is: *If someone questions what I'm doing, can I reasonably justify it?*

Let's say no one answers the door, the lawn is uncut, and there's a large foreclosure notice on the door next to a stack of newspapers. In that case, I'd feel comfortable walking around the house and gathering more information.

If, on the other hand, I'm pretty sure the place is occupied but no one seems to be home, it feels a little dodgy to start peering in the windows.

4. Property Condition and Valuation Clues

Finally, the drive-by is a chance to pick up clues on the current value of the property and the cost to get it ready to sell or rent.

- You'll get a closer look at the actual outside condition of the property. Something may look great from the curb, but as with our fire-damaged home, things can be different up close. After all, only the dents on the front door gave us a clue that there was more to the story than the curb appeal would suggest.

- If someone is home, you'll get, at a minimum, a glimpse at the inside. You might get a sense of the quality of the flooring, for example, or a peek at the condition of the walls or the appliances.
- The drive-by also may give you a chance to talk to either the tenant or the owner. Both are valuable. The current tenant could be your future tenant. Speaking with the owner may even offer you an opportunity to buy the home before auction. In both cases, you'll get a glimpse inside and perhaps even a full tour.

The Best Time for Your Drive-By

Even though it's the house you're interested in—that is, after all, what you're going to buy—it's the presence of *people* that can give you the most information about a property. For example:

- Knocking on the door and meeting the occupant may be an opportunity to meet the owner, get a glimpse inside the house, and perhaps even find a future tenant.
- Seeing cars in the driveway suggests a place is occupied.
- Talking with neighbors can tell you whether a place is occupied, and what the inside looks like.

Of course, the best time to find people at home is evenings and weekends. Plan your drive-by for those times, and you'll learn far more than at any other time.

Drive-By versus Drop-In

We call this step a drive-by, but a better description of our approach would be a "drop-in." There's a huge difference between the information you get by simply driving by and taking photos, versus what you get by going the extra mile and talking to occupants and neighbors. That in-person information will let you avoid obvious risks and accurately price your bid for auction, possibly giving you an edge over your competition.

Still, there's a delicate balance to the drive-by. A home that's being sold at auction is sold "as-is." In theory, the inside condition and occupancy are supposed to be unknown. Yet that inside condition is one of the most important pieces of information about the property. That's why, if you want to do the job right, you need to treat this as a drop-in. You have to knock on doors.

Approaching the house is a gray area. Because the foreclosure is public information, there's nothing stopping anyone from having knowledge of it. And in most neighborhoods, there's no law against walking up and knocking on someone's door.

The key is to be sensitive. An owner going through a foreclosure is going through a tough time. The last thing they need is to feel like the buzzards are circling.

Remember, then, that if you're hiring someone to do your drive-by, *they must be willing to talk to people.* This isn't a job for someone who's too shy to knock on doors and talk to strangers. They also should have the people skills to be sensitive to the homeowners' and tenants' situation.

What Do I Say?

Most people who struggle with the drive-by stage just aren't sure how to start. They don't know what to say when an occupant or a neighbor opens the door.

Our suggestion? *Just be honest.*

Here's what we recommend. You can change the following any way you like so that it feels right for you.

Approaching the property:
Hi, my name is Aaron. Do you live here? There was an online notice that this property was scheduled for foreclosure, and I wanted to confirm that was true.

Approaching the neighboring property:
Hi. Sorry to bother you. My name is Aaron, and I'm wondering if you know whether anyone lives next door.

If you're asked why, simply tell the truth:
There was an online notice that the property was scheduled for foreclosure, and I was trying to confirm that it was vacant. We only buy vacant properties.

Capturing Property Information

Once you look at more than a handful of properties, things start to blur together. Which one had the foundation damage? Was the one on Main Street occupied, or was that the one over on Center Avenue? It takes very little time to forget the innumerable details that you can gather on a single drive-by.

Here are a few important things, then, when it comes to information.

- **Take photos.** They're free, and they're worth a thousand words. Nothing jogs the memory better than photos. Shooting them requires just a few minutes, but the results last forever.
- **Take notes.** Assume that you will remember *nothing*. Jot down what the neighbors tell you as well as your first impressions. List anything that seems relevant.
- **Use Gmail to store it all.** This is my favorite part. For every single address you look at, create a new email using the property address as the subject line. Write all your notes in that email and attach your photos. Send it to a Gmail address you've set up for this purpose. *Voilà!* You now have a permanent and free file system for storing all your property information. You can find the details any time you like simply by searching by address.
- **Consider dedicated software.** There are applications made especially for working with property data. We developed our own app, Prophawk, to capture and store photos and receipts, manage properties, and more. You can find it at www.prophawk.com.

Thanks for mapping!

Keep this email for your records, as it contains the only link to your newly minted map.

Your new map is available here:

https://batchgeo.com/map/b23f978e9f31ef4be643dd7d9486df20

BatchGeo is a free mapping tool that plots large lists of properties on a map to determine your best route for seeing them all.

Gmail is a free tool for tracking drive-by reports. Create a Gmail address just for drive-bys, and email your pictures and notes to that address to stay organized.

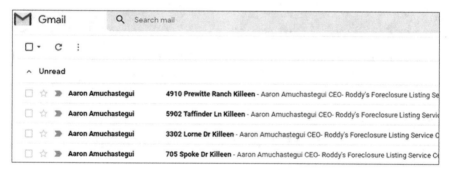

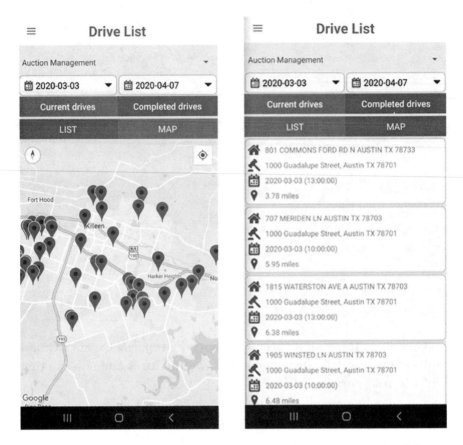

Prophawk.com (Roddy's Portfolio Builder) is a free website and mobile app to track properties, drive inspections, pictures, and more!

A Reminder: Drive-By Information Keeps on Giving

You may be thinking that driving by all these properties is a lot of work, particularly when you're only going to bid on a small percentage of the homes you see.

In the short run, that may be true. But the long run tells a different story. Remember that many of the properties that are slated for auction never make it there. That's why we use the fishing analogy—auctions are a numbers game, and we need to have as many lines in the water as possible.

The biggest reason properties *don't* show up at auction isn't that the foreclosure process has been canceled but that it's been *delayed*. The lender may have granted an extension to the owner. The homeowner may be pursuing legal action to postpone the foreclosure, or they may have settled the outstanding debt, at least for the moment. Regardless, delays are often just that—stalling tactics to put off the inevitable moment when the piper comes to call.

One day in the future, that property you drove by that didn't appear on auction day is going to show up in the hands of the trustee on the courthouse steps. And when it does, *you'll already have the necessary information.*

As you build your database of properties, remember that you may be collecting information that will come in handy for a future auction.

There's No Substitute for a Drive-By

I recently went to an auction in El Paso and noticed that many people were using laptops and tablets to pull up information in real time as the trustees called out addresses.

Looking closer, I understood what I was seeing: They were accessing Google Street View images to see photos of the property. *This,* I realized, *was the first and only time they were seeing the property.*

I could understand the temptation. Street View lets you see a real photo of the house from much the same perspective as someone pulling up in a car. Why, then, not save all that drive-by time and just look online the day of the auction?

Well, I knew why.

As I looked over the shoulder of one bidder, I realized I'd seen the house before. In fact, I would have recognized the address and photo anywhere, because we'd driven by the house every month for a year.

For some of the reasons mentioned earlier, foreclosure kept getting delayed on this home over and over again. Each time it was delayed a month, we stuck to our process, doing our legwork, including *another* drive-by, just to be diligent.

Most months, everything remained the same. Maybe the grass was a little longer or shorter or greener, but there was the house, just sitting there like houses always do.

That is, like houses *almost* always do.

As I stared at the image on the bidder's laptop, I quickly pulled up the file on our software on my phone. There it was—same address. But photos from our most recent drive-by revealed a new and critical fact: the house was *gone*.

Sometime that month, it had been completely demolished. We knew because we'd driven by and taken more photos. The bidder in front of me, who had only dated online information and had never seen the place in person, didn't.

There's no substitute for a good drive-by. I'm not sure whether *that* bidder bought a nonexistent house that day, but I'm pretty confident *someone* did.

All I know for sure is that it wasn't us!

This is 810 Baxter Street in Seguin, TX, showing Google Maps street view two months before auction (on the left), compared to the street view the day before auction (on the right). The property was demolished and it's now an empty lot.

Here's another example of the value of persistent drive-bys. We had been collecting several months' worth of reports on a particular property. One month, a freak accident occurred that impacted the house structurally, mechanically—basically, all the way around. However, by the next month just before auction, the work had been completed, unpermitted, to make the property look better and sell for more.

2 MONTHS BEFORE AUCTION...

THEN BANK FIXES HOUSE RIGHT BEFORE AUCTION...

Roddy's Foreclosure Listing Service

Are you doing your research before auction?

Find the Secret

This chapter began with a look at how a thorough drive-by helped me discover that there'd been a fire in one of the homes we were considering.

There are several lessons to be learned from that story. The first is that even though we call this step a "drive-by," it's so much more than that. Had I simply driven past the address or parked on the street and taken a cursory look around, I would have assumed the home was occupied and well-maintained. I would have estimated it to be in excellent condition, priced it accordingly, and gone to auction. And I would have made a grave mistake.

That's the obvious lesson: A good drive-by can help you avoid significant risks at auction.

Remember, however, what we know about risks—they can be

managed. Upon discovering that there'd been a fire in the house, I could have simply been grateful for my diligent drive-by, then moved on as fast as my feet would carry me. I could have settled for avoiding a big risk.

Instead, I took the time to dig a little deeper. And, as it does with so many aspects of buying foreclosures at auction, the extra due diligence paid off.

The closer I looked that day, the more I became convinced that the fire hadn't really been that bad. Rather than completely discard the property, I decided to adjust my bidding price to better reflect the work we'd have to do to restore the home.

On auction day at the courthouse, it turned out to be no big secret that there had been a fire at the property. The other experienced buyers had done enough homework, and the word was out: This place was one big red flag. But I had seen it for myself and looked as closely as I could. I thought the fire wasn't horrible, figuring that with some work, we could really do something with the place.

My up-close analysis gave me an extra edge. That day at auction, no one really wanted to bid. We secured the place for a price that allowed plenty of room for renovations, and in the end, the property worked out great. We had to repaint everything and use a fire restoration company to get the smoky smell out, but the deal was profitable for us—so much so that we bought a second fire-damaged property not long after.

LESSON: A great drive-by isn't just about avoiding risk. It's about uncovering advantage.

We had a similar experience with a property that was frequently postponed at auction.

The first time we drove by, it was clearly occupied, and we knew we'd have to adjust our bid price to compensate for eviction costs.

Foreclosure was postponed, but we continued to drive by the property each month. About six months in, we discovered it was unoccupied but a little trashed. We changed our maximum bid accordingly, and the auction was delayed again.

After a couple more months, we saw that something had changed. Now there were cars in the driveway, and the lawn was freshly mown. The place looked great. *Occupied*, we thought.

Still, we took the time to talk to the neighbors again. We learned that *they* had cleaned up the lot and were parking their cars there, not new tenants. The house was still vacant!

That little extra knowledge allowed us to pay a bit more than the other bidders at auction, who all believed the place was occupied.

A good drive-by is about being thorough, yes. But it's also about being persistent. It's about being willing to knock on doors, ask questions, have conversations. A good drive-by means having the character to do more than the next guy.

It's that *more* that will give you an edge on auction day.

CHAPTER 6

STEP 3: PROPERTY ANALYSIS
How to Find the Magic Number

So far, you've completed two out of our five steps.

In Step 1, you created (or purchased) a list of properties scheduled to be sold at auction, and then filtered that list to meet your most basic requirements for things like price, age, and location.

In Step 2, you drove by (or had someone else drive by) each house to gather more information. As with the previous step, you then filtered your list further, excluding properties based on new factors like occupancy and the condition of the home.

Now you should now have a much shorter list of properties. Every house on that list should share one common element: You'd love to buy it auction...*if* the price is right.

But what *is* the right price? We still know very little about these homes financially. When you're standing on the courthouse steps on auction day, how will you know how much to bid? Bid too much, and you run the risk of losing money. Cap your bid too low, and you might not buy anything at all. Neither is an outcome you can sustain for long in the foreclosure business.

The solution is to find each property's *magic number*—the maximum you'd be willing to bid at auction that still allows room for your desired profit.

By the end of this chapter, that's what you'll be able to do. For any potential listing, you'll be ready to distill everything you know about the property down to one all-important number: the highest amount you're willing to pay.

Property Analysis: The Big Picture

In the broadest sense, you need to know only two things to figure out your maximum bid: how much you can sell the property for once you've fixed it up, and how much all that fixing is going to cost. When you subtract the second from the first, you get your maximum bid.

Resale Price – Cost = Max Bid

Of course, that's a simplified equation. The resale price might be just one number, but there are many costs on the road to resale, such as:

- **Realtor commissions.** You'll pay a Realtor a percentage of the selling price.
- **Construction costs.** These may include money spent on demolition, cleaning, painting, flooring, HVAC repairs, lawn care, and more.
- **Past-due taxes.** Any back taxes will have to be paid to the county.
- **Occupancy costs.** Evicting a tenant or finding a new one carries a price tag.
- **Closing costs.** You'll incur legal and other expenses to finalize the deal.
- **Liens.** Liens are costs recorded against the property that were incurred by prior owners. Many liens will go away after foreclosure, but some will need to be paid. Different types of liens include mechanics liens, federal tax liens, and city utility liens. A lien could also be a warning of a lawsuit, which will cost to remedy.
- **Miscellaneous overhead.** This includes expenditures leading up to the auction, such as fees for drivers and title companies, plus various expenses related to property ownership—insurance, security, banking, and more.

And let's not forget one more magic piece of the puzzle:
- **Desired profit.** After all this, you want to make sure *you* get paid, too. Most investors want to make a 10 to 20 percent return on their

upfront investment. We'll add that to our equation as well; otherwise, your max bid will be just enough to pay everyone else except you!

It's time, then, to expand our original equation to include more specifics on the cost side. Here it is again, in more detail:

Resale Price
−   Realtor commissions
     Construction costs
     Past-due taxes
     Liens
     Occupancy costs
     Closing costs
     Miscellaneous overhead
     Desired profit

=   Max Bid

We now have what we call our *bid calculator*. Once you fill in all the blanks, you'll know the maximum amount you should bid at auction to both cover your costs and make a tidy return on the property.

> **NOTE:** You can download a spreadsheet version of this bid calculator at **BiggerPockets.com/ForeclosureBonus**.

The rest of this chapter is a step-by-step breakdown of how to come up with these numbers. To keep things simple, we're going to split the chapter into two parts. Part A will look at how to estimate the resale price (the first number), while part B will examine how to calculate the various costs of getting the property ready for resale (all the other numbers).

A. RESALE PRICE

Our starting point is the "top line" number in our previous calculation—the resale price. That's the amount you believe you can sell the house for after you've taken possession and done any necessary work. In other words, when everything has been completed, from repainting the walls to replacing the light fixtures and paying the people who help, how much will the house sell for on the open market?

The answer, as any real estate professional knows, is: *It depends*.

It depends on the location. It depends on the house's amenities. It depends on the market and the economy. It depends on the surrounding properties. The value of any house depends on a *lot*.

This can be a challenge even for seasoned real estate professionals. Fortunately, a system has gradually been developed to tease out what an individual home is worth.

Fundamentally, that system is about market value, and its premise is this: **If other houses have sold in the neighborhood recently and those houses are similar to the one in question, then the house in question will probably sell for a similar amount, all other things being equal.**

These similar houses are called *comparables*, or comps for short, and they represent the key to coming up with a number for the resale value of the house you're considering. If you can find evidence of other houses that have sold that are similar, you can use those numbers to help find *your* number.

Now that you've narrowed down your spreadsheet of possible properties to just those that fit your goals, you can go through the following steps with each one.

1. Take a Bird's-Eye View

Your first step is to get a big-picture view of the house in question. The best tool for this job is Google Maps, which will allow you to see the property you're interested in, plus the surrounding area. Make sure to check not just the map view, but also the satellite view, which lets you see actual images of the area.

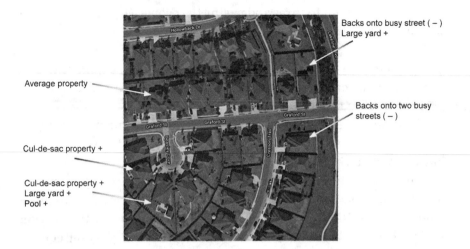

Backs onto busy street (–)
Large yard +

Average property

Backs onto two busy streets (–)

Cul-de-sac property +

Cul-de-sac property +
Large yard +
Pool +

The question you're trying to answer at this point is: How typical is the house I'm looking at? To do that, consider the following factors:

- **Front and rear exposure.** Does it back onto a forest? A lake? Other yards? Power lines? Does it face a typical residential street or a busy main throughway?
- **Relative size.** Is it significantly larger or smaller than average?
- **Lot size.** Is the lot similar in size and shape to the nearby lots?
- **Amenities.** Is your house the only one with a pool? The only one without? Is it the only one without a garage?
- **Neighboring properties.** Does your house have atypical neighbors, such as commercial spaces, industrial units, or empty lots?

Note any of these differences on your spreadsheet. Remember that every house is different. That's why this is a bird's-eye view. You don't want to get lost in the weeds by, say, examining which house has the most trees in the front yard. Focus on the big picture.

> **Note:** If the property you're considering seems significantly different from those in the surrounding area, see the "Help!" section later in this chapter.

2. Look for Sales History and Comparable Properties

Once you've established that your house is similar to the others around it, it's time to start looking for your comps—houses that have sold recently and are similar to the one you're interested in.

For that, we're going to make use of one or more of the real estate data sites, such as Zillow, Redfin, and Realtor.com—the same sites you used in the latter stages of list-building in Step 1.

Choosing which site to use as your preferred source will mostly depend on what county you're living in. You'll have to experiment to find the one with the best sales data for your area. (It's worth noting that a licensed real estate professional will usually have access to more data than the aggregator sites. If you are a Realtor or you know one who can help, you'll have an advantage. This also holds true if your county's sales data isn't public or you live outside the United States.)

To get started, simply search for the address of the home on your preferred site. The results should look familiar, since you did the same thing in Step 1. This time, however, you're going to be doing two things differently. First, you'll be digging deeper into the history on this particular home to look for sales, listings, or any other recent activity. Second, you'll be looking at *other* houses that you might be able to use as comps.

Data for Your Property

Scan the listing for your property and look first for any relevant listing or sales activity. Note the dates. What we're hoping for at this stage is **to get lucky and find recent sales activity that would help us close in on a resale value.** For example:

- A listing followed by a quick sale is an indication that the price was close to or perhaps below market value.
- Conversely, a listing that has languished with no sales activity or with repeated price drops may indicate that the price is above market value.

For example, if your house was listed for $175,000 and sat on the market for six months, that price probably did not reflect the home's market value. After all, market value is *what the market is willing to pay.* In this case, the market wasn't willing to pay $175,000.

Next, while you're looking at the sales history for this particular property, make sure you've noted key factors, like square footage, age, number of bedrooms, and number of baths. Add anything new to your spreadsheet. You're going to use that info as your base criteria for finding comparable properties in the local market.

Address	Status	Price	Bed	Bath	SF
99 Ames	My Property	????	3	2	1525

Data for Comparable Properties

Remember the valuation principle: If you can find similar properties that have sold, you can use those to estimate the value of your subject property (the one you're interested in at auction).

Your chosen real estate site will usually do a good job of showing you properties for sale in the neighborhood. A great comp meets three criteria:

- It's close to your subject property.
- It's similar to your subject property in size, age, features, rooms, and finishes.
- It has sold in the past ninety days.

To get a good idea of value, you want to find at least three comps. That won't always be easy, but that's your goal. More is better!

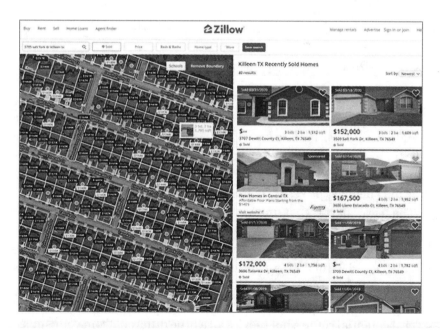

When you find a comparable property, add it to a spreadsheet that captures the following:

- Address
- Selling price
- Square footage
- Number of bedrooms
- Number of bathrooms
- Any additional comments, for example: "high-quality finishes" or "backs onto highway"

I usually start a new spreadsheet, add the subject property to the top, and then add the comps above it.

Address	Status	Price	Bed	Bath	SF	DOM	Date	Built	Comments
194 Ames	Pending	$225,000	3	2	1469	13	2/13/20	2009	Recent Remodel- Nice
238 Goddard	Pending	$195,000	3	2	1323	1	10/17/19	2012	Recent Remodel- Nice
195 Musgrav	Sold	$193,500	3	2	1795	9	9/27/19	2004	Needed work, older home
112 Jerngan	Sold	$215,000	3	2	1476	27	10/10/19	2014	Nice home
183 Musgrav	Sold	$198,500	3	2	1929	34	9/30	2004	Foreclosure by bank
147 Langely	Sold	$197,500	3	2	1411	54	11/22/19	2004	Older home
125 Wallops	Sold	$246,000	3	2	2096	13	4/3/20	2014	Good condition
100 Wallops	Pending	$258,000	4	2	2096	5	3/18/2020	2014	Pool
256 Voss	Active	$289,875	3	2	2327	39	3/2/2020	2016	2 story
99 Ames	My Property	????	3	2	1525			2014	

If you find three or more sales in the past three months that are close by and very similar to the property you're interested in, congratulations! Take the average of their selling prices, and you've got yourself a reasonable estimate as to what your place will sell for. **Enter it in the top line of your bid sheet as the *resale value*.**

The tricky part is that finding three identical properties nearby that have sold isn't always easy. Houses are rarely identical. Even in cookie-cutter communities, houses that have identical floor plans and look exactly the same from the outside will have different cabinets, appliances, flooring, and fixtures on the inside.

The most realistic situation you're going to face, then, is that you find several potential comps, but they're all a little different from your subject property. One might be bigger than yours. Another could be a lot nicer inside. The third one might be ten years older.

In the example above, we were comparing apples to apples. Now you've got a trickier situation involving mixed fruit. What do you do? You try to make your comps, on paper, look just like yours—you turn the oranges and grapefruits into apples. It's a process we call *making adjustments*.

3. Adjust Your Comparables

Even though your list of comparables may not be very...ahem, *comparable*, it's still the best information you have to build your guess about the value of the subject property.

To use those comparables, however, you'll have to *adjust* them so that they more closely resemble the property you're trying to value. For example:

- A nearby sale, let's call it Property A, is 1,800 square feet, but yours is 1,500. How much should you adjust the sales price of Property A to make it closer to yours?
- Another nearby sale, Property B, has much nicer finishes inside. How much should you adjust the sales price to make it a better match for yours?
- Property C has three bedrooms, while yours has two. How should you adjust the sales price?

Adjustments are tricky. They're as much art as science, and the single biggest factor in becoming good at them is simply experience—specifically, the experience that comes from looking at a lot of *sold* real estate.

That's why, when you speak with a Realtor, they'll be able to say, "Oh. That one sold for $300,000, but it had the nice cabinets and the bonus room over the garage. Yours will likely sell for $265,000."

It's not magic; they just have enough market experience to be better at guessing.

And that's the lesson: *Everyone is guessing*. You're just trying to become a good guesser, which takes practice.

> **LESSON:** Estimating value is an educated guessing game, and the best guessers are the people who see the most sales data. The more often you can look at sales in your auction area, the better you'll become!

Still, we can make an attempt to standardize some adjustments. It's not perfect, and there are many ways in which these adjustments can be wrong, but you might find them helpful at the start.

Some Common Changes to a Property to Adjust Value:

(This would work for an average price point of around $150,000 to $250,000.) Adjustments would be smaller for less expensive homes and larger for more expensive homes.

- **Backs onto Busy Road:** Subtract $5,000 per lane
- **Private Cul-de-sac:** Add $10,000 to $15,000
- **Recently Painted and Updated:** Add $5 per square foot
- **Badly in Need of Paint and Updating** *(Common for bank-listed fore-closures)*: Subtract $5 per square foot
- **Swimming Pool:** Add $10,000 to $30,000
- **High-End Finishes** *(Granite, stainless, new cabinets)*: Add $5 per square foot
- **Large Yard:** Add $5,000 to $20,000
- **Single Story:** Add $10,000
- **Gated Community:** Add $10,000 if comps are outside gate

Another way to approach adjustments is to find two comps that are fairly similar to *each other*, except for one attribute. For example, two nearly identical homes have sold in the past three months. The only meaningful difference is that one has an extra bedroom. In this case, the difference in the selling price gives us an excellent idea as to the value of one bedroom. Now you can use that per-bedroom value to adjust other comps.

- If a comp has one bedroom *more* than your house, you'll have to *subtract* that bedroom value from the comp to make it more like your subject property.
- Likewise, if a comp has one bedroom *less* than yours, you'll have to *add* that value to the comp to make it more like the one you're interested in.

Do this for all your comps, making adjustments for size, bedrooms, baths, etc. Once you're satisfied that you've "equalized" your comps with your subject property, you can average their values for a good estimate of what yours might sell for.

Valuation Example

To get you started, let's look at an example. We'll start with a real subject property and go through the process.

With the list of comparable sales below, there is a big difference between older home sales prices and newer ones, so I select the three properties closest in size to my property that were recently built.

Address	Status	Price	Bed	Bath	SF	DOM	Date	Built	Comments
194 Ames	Pending	$225,000	3	2	1469	13	2/13/20	2009	Recent Remodel- Nice
238 Goddard	Pending	$195,000	3	2	1323	1	10/17/19	2012	Recent Remodel- Nice
195 Musgrav	Sold	$193,500	3	2	1795	9	9/27/19	2004	Needed work, older home
112 Jerngan	Sold	$215,000	3	2	1476	27	10/10/19	2014	Nice home
183 Musgrav	Sold	$198,500	3	2	1929	34	9/30	2004	Foreclosure by bank
147 Langely	Sold	$197,500	3	2	1411	54	11/22/19	2004	Older home
125 Wallops	Sold	$246,000	3	2	2096	13	4/3/20	2014	Good condition
100 Wallops	Pending	$258,000	4	2	2096	5	3/18/2020	2014	Pool
256 Voss	Active	$289,875	3	2	2327	39	3/2/2020	2016	2 story
99 Ames	My Property	????	3	2	1525			2014	

Next, I adjust each of them based on how they compare to my property. Then I take the average of the three after adjustments:

Address	Status	Price	Bed	Bath	SF	DOM	Date	Built	Comments	Adjust	My Value
194 Ames	Pending	$225,000	3	2	1469	13	2/13/20	2009	Mine slightly larger	7000	232000
238 Goddard	Pending	$195,000	3	2	1323	1	10/17/19	2012	Larger, market higher Now	20000	215000
112 Jerngan	Sold	$215,000	3	2	1476	27	10/10/19	2014	Larger, market higher Now	15000	230000
										AVG	$225,667
99 Ames	My Property	$225,667	3	2	1525			2014			

The Dangers of Square-Foot Pricing

One of the challenges you'll discover early on when looking for comparables is that houses that have sold nearby are rarely the same size.

From the street, some communities really do seem to be cookie-cutter similar. But that's less common than it appears. While some developments consist only of houses that follow the same footprint and layout, it's more likely that your comps will be similar in many ways but different in square footage.

For example, when trying to come up with a price for 256 Voss Street, a 2,327-square-foot home, I see a sold house on the same street just a few doors down. The house at 113 Voss Street sold for $218,000 and is 1,467 square feet.

At this point, the first thing that comes to mind is: *If only these were the same size, I'd have perfect comps.* The second thing will be: *Hey. Why don't I figure out the price per square foot—then I can calculate the value of ANY house!*

So you grab a house from the middle of the pile and do the math. *Let's see, $218,000 for 1,467 square feet. That's $149 per square foot. I'm a genius!*

You wouldn't be alone in thinking this—many a real estate professional has done the same thing. But, like them, you'd be mistaken.

A 1,467-square-foot house that recently sold for $218,000 is indeed worth $149 per square foot. But it's a mistake to use that $149 multiplier to estimate the value of larger or smaller houses. Why? Because the price per square foot doesn't rise in lockstep with the increase in size.

		Price	SF	Price/SF
113 Voss St	Sold	$218,000.00	1467	$148.60
256 Voss St	Proposed:	$345,798.23	2327	$148.60

You can't easily see from the numbers what's going on here, so let's graph the data and include the rest of the comps on the street.

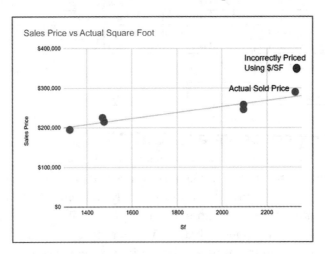

Address	Status		Price	Bed	Bath	SF		DOM	Date	Built	Comments
194 Ames	Pending	Sold	$225,000	3	2	1469	$153	13	2/13/20	2009	Recent Remodel- Nice
238 Goddard	Pending	Sold	$195,000	3	2	1323	$147	1	10/17/19	2012	Recent Remodel- Nice
112 Jerngan	Sold	Sold	$215,000	3	2	1476	$146	27	10/10/19	2014	Nice home
125 Wallops	Sold	Sold	$246,000	3	2	2096	$117	13	4/3/20	2014	Good condition
100 Wallops	Pending	Sold	$258,000	4	2	2096	$123	5	3/18/2020	2014	Pool

Now you can see that that, while our 1,467-square-foot house is indeed worth $149 per square foot, a larger house is not priced proportionally. Our 2,327 square feet actually is worth $125 per square foot, not $149.

So you can't use a standard square-foot multiplier to figure out value—but there is a point at which it can be helpful.

If, after adjusting for other things like finishes and location and condition, you come up with a value, you can check that value against your square footage graph as a way to double-check your results.

Let's say, for example, that your subject property is 1,800 square feet. You don't have a comp that's the same size, but you do have a *range* of comps—the same ones we graph above.

If you've come up with a value for your subject property, you can plot it on the graph and then simply eyeball it. Does it fit on the imaginary line connecting the properties? Is it close?

This is a rough tool, but if your valuation is way off, that's a reason to double-check your work. In the example below, we don't have any comps near 1,800 square feet, but if you plot on the line, you can estimate a sales price of around $235,000

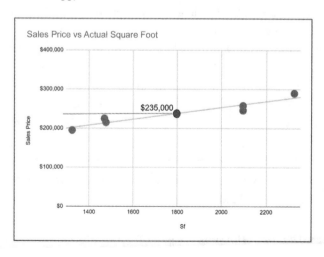

B. COSTS

In Part A, you found the estimated resale value of a home—which is the top line in our bid calculator:

Resale Price
(–) Realtor commissions
Construction costs
Past-due taxes
Liens
Occupancy costs
Closing costs
Miscellaneous overhead
Desired profit

_____

= MAX BID

That's the amount we expect to receive on a sale. From that, we need to subtract all the other line items.

Consistent Line Items

Several of these items are consistent from property to property, or relatively easy to find. Let's tackle them first.

- **Realtor commissions.** Your agent will take 3 to 4 percent of the selling price. Multiply your resale price by .04 and enter the amount.
- **Past-due taxes.** You should already have them on file from your title search. Enter the amount.
- **Occupancy costs.** Occupied houses tend to have higher costs associated with them. We like to allow an extra 5 percent for occupancy costs, such as legal fees or cash for keys (more on this later). Add it in.
- **Closing costs.** We generally use 2 percent of the resale price, assuming ninety days' worth of taxes, plus title and insurance costs. Add it to your bid sheet.
- **Desired profit.** Most investors want a 10 to 20 percent return. Again, multiply the resale price by the profit (.10 to .20) and enter the value in the bid sheet.

That leaves two items that are a little less cut-and-dried.

Miscellaneous Overhead

There are always costs you don't see coming. Most are small, but they can add up. Staff overhead is particularly important to track. If you're paying for drive-bys, title checks, or broker price opinions, your costs are going to be higher.

The trick here is that the overhead applies to *all* the houses you look at, not just the one you buy. If you pay someone to drive by 40 houses in order to buy one at auction, that cost needs to be absorbed by the house you buy, but if you apply the 40-house cost of everything to all the bids, you're going to have max bids that are unreasonably high.

There's no clear answer here. If you do everything yourself and you buy one home per year at auction, then your overhead may be just your time and the cost of your car, which you'd enter on the bid sheet. If, however, you're using other services and buying several houses, you'll need to think through the math more carefully. The point is this: There are a number of costs that are not covered in the other lines on the bid sheet. Track *everything* you spend, and then allocate it here in a way that fits your approach.

Construction Costs

Like resale value, construction costs vary from house to house and can be complicated to estimate. Here are some *very rough* estimates of the costs of various renovation line items. If you have renovation experience or know a contractor, that will help. If not, the following will give you a place to start.

- **Secure house and rekey:** $250 to $300
- **Trash-out interior and exterior:** $0 to $3,000
- **Power wash:** $250
- **Landscape cleanup:** $250 to $3,000
- **Exterior detailing:** $200 to thousands of dollars, depending on dry rot repairs, light fixtures, siding, stucco, etc.
- **Exterior paint:** $1 to $2 per square foot
- **Interior paint prep:** $0 to $500
- **Interior paint:** $1 to $3 per square foot
- **Interior detailing:** $500 to $1,000
- **Window replacement:** $400 per window
- **Flooring installation:** $1 to $3 per square foot

- **Appliance order/installation:** $1,000 per set for base level, but can become tens of thousands for higher end models. Average base level is $500 for range, $350 for dishwasher, and $250 for microwave/hood combo
- **HVAC service:** $250 to $3,000
- **Deep cleaning:** $250 to $500
- **Carpet cleaning:** $250 to $700

One of the most convenient rules of thumb I know for estimating renovation costs is to assume that the cost of materials is roughly equal to the cost of labor to install/use them.

This is an extremely liberating rule. It means you can go to your local building supply store, add up the cost of the materials to do a job (no skill required), and use that as an estimate of the labor costs. For example, if a ceiling fan costs $150 to buy, you can assume the cost of installation might be similar—$150. Total cost? $300.

Like our other shortcuts, this is not 100 percent accurate, but it has served me well over the years and will give you a starting point until you have the experience to make more educated guesses.

The Danger of Magnifying Costs

As you start to go through the costing exercise, you'll notice two things. First, there's often a *range*—a low end and a high end. Second, you might be tempted to always use the high number, *just to be safe*.

The problem with this approach is that you end up with a sky-high total for your construction costs, and one that probably isn't realistic in most cases.

A better solution is to use a spreadsheet with two cost columns—one for the low end and one for the high. Add each column to get a total estimate for both low *and* high end. Then average the two to get a more reasonable number.

Back to the Bid Sheet

You should now have a line item for every blank on the bid sheet. Once you do the final math, you're left with one magic number: your maximum bid on auction day!

BID SHEET

Address
....
121 Main St

Resale Price		$125,000
(–) Realtor Commission (3-6% of resale) - Multiply by resale	(125000X.04)	$5,000
(–) Estimated Construction		$15,000
(–) Past-Due Prop Taxes	From County Website	$1,250
(–) Closing Costs (2% of sales assumes 90 days taxes, title, insurance)	(125000X.02)	$2,500
(–) Desired Profit	Usually 10% to 20% of investment	$10,000
Max Bid	125000 5000 15000 1250 2500 10000	$91,250

That number, as you'll see in future chapters, is your big red STOP sign. It's the most you're willing to pay for the house.

Help!

Some houses are easy to analyze. They're in cookie-cutter communities with lots of recent sales. In those cases, one house is often much like another, and there are plenty of comparables. You might make some small adjustments for square footage or interior finishes, but the job of coming up with the resale value number is fairly simple.

Other houses are much trickier. You might find there are no comps or that the houses vary widely. It's difficult to find apples to compare to apples.

What should you do when the adjustments are too hard to make, and you feel like you're truly just taking a stab in the dark at the valuation?

You have a few options.

1. Professional Appraisals

There are, of course, people who specialize in assessing resale value. They're called appraisers, and they're usually trained and certified for exactly what you're struggling to learn. The upside is that they're fast, accurate, and have a ton of market experience. The downside is that you have to pay for each appraisal, generally from a few hundred bucks to more than a thousand, depending on the area.

As with many costs in this process, that may not seem like much for a single property, but if you have to do a dozen professional appraisals in order to bid on one house, the costs add up.

2. Online Data Aggregators

Another option is to use the valuations from some of the real estate property sites. If Zillow's price estimate is x, for example, while Redfin's is y, you could average them or pick the one that seems more accurate or conservative.

In our experience, this can work, but you can't always rely on the number you get. Sites like Zillow and Redfin are limited by the same things you are—if there are no comps, there are no comps. It's hard to put a market value on something when there's no market.

3. Broker Price Opinions

A third option is to work with a real estate professional. Most experienced brokers and agents have looked at *thousands* of comps and put resale value estimates on hundreds of homes. They know the market and some will have decades of experience watching it. A great agent with local experience can tell you in seconds what a house will sell for.

We call these *broker price opinions*, and they represent a middle ground between the previous two options. The valuation may be more accurate and informed than what you'd find online yourself, but it won't be free, at least not for long or in volume. Typically, an agent won't do this repeatedly out of the goodness of their heart.

Some brokerages have a standard fee for this. Other times, you'll need to find some way to reward an agent who agrees to help, for example:

- Offer to give them the listing if you are successful at auction.
- Partner with them. You're the foreclosure and auction expert; they're the real estate brain.
- Pay them a per-value estimate. You may be able to arrange a fee-for-service arrangement with an agent to help with valuations.

Much of the above also applies to calculating construction costs. Some houses are easier than others. When we bought a fire-damaged house at auction, we had to do some extra legwork to figure out how much it was going to cost to remove the smell of smoke and assess any structural damage. It was daunting, to say the least.

Fortunately, we had lots of construction experience, but if we didn't, we'd likely have worked with local contractors to help us figure out some of the numbers in exchange for the likelihood of doing the work if we were successful at auction.

The Art of Analysis

Still, for all the tips, analyzing a property can seem like an impossibly complicated task. How do you find information from the disparate worlds of demographics, construction, real estate, and finance? And how do you combine them to come up with a valuation you can use to go to auction?

If it feels overwhelming, consider this:

- **Help is out there.** You can use a Realtor. You can subscribe to services like Padhawk that help with data. You can speak to contractors. Revisit Chapter 3, on assembling your team.
- **You will surprise yourself.** Time, and your brain, tend to do amazing things. You may be overwhelmed on your first visit to Realtor.com or in your first attempts to figure out the cost to renovate a home. But with every attempt you make, with every property you try to analyze, you're gradually building experience.
- **You don't have to go to auction *tomorrow*.** No one is forcing you to

buy something at the next auction. Take your time. Allow yourself to build knowledge, connections, and experience. And when you're ready, go for it!

Remember that, over time, *you* are going to become a minor expert in all these things. You won't always need someone else's help. For example, you might start with an agent and then realize that you don't need them, or that you need them only for atypical or tricky properties. You might need a contractor to help you work through costing on a couple of places, and then realize you know enough to do it on your own.

As with all things foreclosure-related, you're going to learn more than you think, faster than you think!

CHAPTER 7
STEP 4: TITLE REVIEW
Do a Background Check on Your Shortlist

Imagine you're searching for someone to do an extremely important job in your life. Maybe you need a nanny for your children or a financial advisor. Perhaps you're choosing a surgeon to perform a critical medical procedure.

Clearly, this is a decision you really want to get right. As your list of candidates shortens, you feel the pressure rising. The stakes are high.

What do you do?

Like everyone else, you do your homework. You do a background check on the final candidates. You call their references. You look them up online. You verify their bona fides. It's the last step to ensure you haven't missed anything along the way. Doing due diligence before making important decisions is what lets you sleep well at night once you've made your choice.

Buying at auction is no different. The stakes—your hard-earned cash—can be high. Investing in a property with problems is like hiring a person with problems—at some point, you're going to pay a steep price.

To mitigate the risks, real estate comes with its own type of background check called a *title review*. It's the last step in our process. After you've narrowed your initial list of many possible foreclosure properties down to a handful of good prospects, title check is your final piece of due diligence before you head to the courthouse to bid.

What Is Title?

If you want to sell the pair of shoes you bought at the mall to a friend, no one really cares. You can sell them, give them away, or throw them out any time you like. It's a simple transaction.

Not so with real estate. High-value assets like houses and cars have an extra layer of complexity when they are bought and sold. It's called "title," which is a fancy name for someone's *rights* to a piece of property. Having title gives you the legal right to do with a house what you would with a smaller asset, like that pair of Converse hanging around your closet. Clear title lets you sell, reassign, or finance a piece of real estate—it puts it fully under your control, within the limits of the law.

That's the kind of reassurance we're looking for when we go to auction.

Lien on Me

Here's where things get tricky. Title in real estate is particularly important because homes are often *collateralized*—they're used as a way to borrow money or extend services. The most common way of collateralizing real estate is through a mortgage.

When you borrow money to buy a house, the bank stakes a claim against your property in the form of a *lien*. If you don't pay the mortgage, the rights provided by the lien allow the bank to take possession of your home and sell it to clear the debt—the exact process we described earlier that led poor Dave to foreclosure.

A mortgage, however, isn't the only way that a lien or other encumbrance can be connected to real estate. Property taxes, contractor work, lawsuits, and more can all result in claims against a property, dividing and complicating the title.

Title, then, isn't just a piece of paper. It's the collection of rights that you, as the new property owner, are entitled to. Without clear title, you're exposed to higher risk and may be limited in what you can do with your property in the future.

The Auction Difference

When you buy a house the typical way—through a licensed real estate agent on the open market—there's an established process for sorting out title and making sure you fully understand your rights and obligations.

In general, after a seller accepts your offer to buy their home, the real estate agent retains a title search company to go through the necessary public records and look for liens or other complications related to the property. They're watching closely for anything that might impact your right to manage your asset as you see fit.

A title search might uncover any number of things, such as:

- Unpaid property taxes
- Other financial liens
- Pending lawsuits
- Boundary/border issues, such as a fence or building that encroaches on a neighboring property
- Complications with estates and heirs
- Mistakes and improper paperwork errors with previous title transfers

The title company examines all of these and provides you with a tidy little report that sums up the legal history of the property with respect to ownership, liens, taxes, and other possible encumbrances, and gives an exact legal description of the property. Any red flags will be clearly identified, plus you get title insurance, just in case they missed anything.

It's all simple, clear, and gives everyone peace of mind for a small fee.

Buying at auction, however, is a different story.

The timelines of auctions generally mean that a title search company can help, but they won't guarantee their work—in most cases, there isn't enough time for them to do the in-depth digging required to offer title insurance. That, in turn, means it's usually not worth paying a title company fee for every property you want to bid on.

It's a conundrum. Understanding title is critical, but the pros can't necessarily give you what you want. What to do?

Three Ways to Do Title Review

There are three ways to approach title review for the properties on your shortlist. There are pros and cons to each, but we have a recommended approach for your first time around.

1. Pay a Title Company

As mentioned, you can use a title company to review the auction properties you're interested in, but you won't get a guarantee. This isn't the same as a title report—it's a much lower cost version. We're not saying you shouldn't use a title company—more on that below—but you should consider this a "buyer beware" situation.

Using a title company for an auction research role instead of a title report means you're (a) paying someone to do a job that they don't necessarily have the time to do properly, and (b) allowing them to do it with no guarantees. That certainly opens the door to a less-than-thorough job. The advantage, though, is cost. A regular title report can cost as much as $2,000, which would not be profitable for 50 houses per auction when you are hoping to buy just one. A limited review, on the other hand, costs $30 to $50.

While the services of a title company are not free, their experts are the pros. The information you get from them, even if not guaranteed, is likely to be strong.

2. DIY

You can absolutely learn to do title review yourself, and that's what the rest of this chapter will focus on. On the plus side, you'll save a little money, but you'll pay a price in the time you're going to spend doing it.

The real value in the DIY approach is twofold. First, you're going to get an education—you'll start to truly understand the liens and encumbrances and other possible challenges that can arise with title. The second, and arguably greater benefit, however, is that *no one cares about title as much as you do*. It is, after all, your money that's on the line at auction.

3. Hire/Train Someone to Do It for You

The DIY approach also allows for a third option. Once you have a solid understanding of how to do a complete title review, you can teach someone *else* to do it in exactly the way you want it done.

It's the best of both worlds—you're not doing all the work, but you're not handing the review over to someone who may not be incentivized to give you the best results.

Where should you start? Our recommendation is to begin the same way we did: Do it yourself *and* pay a title company. We call it double coverage, and it's an approach that gives you some great advantages:

- **You get to compare your results against the pros'.** Did you miss something? Comparing your title discoveries against those of a title company is a great way to find the holes in your search. And when you stop seeing holes, you'll know you're getting good.

- **No one cares like you do.** Your due diligence, when your money is on the line, versus the due diligence of a title company that doesn't have to guarantee your results, is no contest, motivation-wise. You win, hands down. Double coverage keeps you engaged, at least until you find someone you trust to help.
- **You'll truly understand the properties you're looking at.** Every property has a history, and some of them can be quite complicated. Properties change hands. They are financed and refinanced. People get sued. People die and their heirs fight with each other and fight with the neighbors. Title research tells you the story of the asset you're buying, and that makes you a better investor. Double coverage means you have a pro to help when you encounter weird cases and complications.

In summary, title research matters and there's a lot of value in learning to do it yourself. The good news is this: It's not that hard to learn. Much like buying at auction, successful title research is a process. All you need to do is follow the correct steps. In this chapter, we'll show you our process for careful title research that ensures three things:

- **Free and clear title.** When you buy a property at auction, you want to be able to make smart decisions afterward. You want full control. You may want to sell the property. You may want to rent it or refinance it. Knowing that you have control over those decisions is critical.
- **No nasty surprises.** In the worst-case scenario, you can lose all your money at auction by not doing your due diligence on title. Those bad surprises are painful to go through, and they're almost always expensive.
- **Accurate bid pricing.** Uncovering issues with title doesn't mean you shouldn't buy a property at auction. What it does mean is that you'll need to adjust your final calculations accordingly. Are there unpaid property taxes, for example? Those will need to be settled, and you'll want to take that amount into account. Good title review makes for good auction bidding!

The Task at Hand: Find and Prioritize Surviving Title Risks

Although we commonly speak of buying *properties* at auction and foreclosing on *houses*, that language isn't technically accurate.

When you bid on the courthouse steps, what you're really trying to buy is a *loan* that someone has defaulted on—it's *loans* that are foreclosed on, not houses.

All loans, however, are not created equal.

In Chapter 1 we met Dave, who fell further and further behind on his home mortgage payments until eventually his loan was foreclosed on, and his house was sold at auction.

You know now that the reason the mortgage holder (the bank) was able to take Dave's house was because it registered a lien against the property. The lien gave the bank a legal interest in Dave's property. When Dave failed to pay, the bank used that legal stake in Dave's home to repossess it and sell it (to an investor like you) to recover their money.

But here's where things get interesting. If you're going to start buying up loans at auction—remember, that's what you're doing, because it's *loans* that are foreclosed on—you need to understand the loan you're buying.

Why? Because:

- **There can be more than one lien against a property.** From mortgage liens and mechanic's liens to tax liens and beyond, the bank may not be the only one out there with an interest in a property.
- **Not all liens are equal in priority.** A first mortgage, for example, takes priority over a second. We like to buy first-position loans.
- **Not all liens "survive" foreclosure.** Some obligations are erased when the property is sold at auction. Those we can ignore!

Any registered claim involving the title of a property is something that can impact your profitability, and the job of title review is to find those claims and assess their impact.

We've broken title review into three steps to make it easier:

1. **Check for outstanding property taxes.** This is relatively straightforward. Outstanding property taxes almost always have to be paid, so we like to sort that out first.
2. **Find any other encumbrances.** I call these the L's—liens, lawsuits, and liabilities. This includes anything that might interfere with clear title or cost you extra money after auction.

3. **Filter and prioritize your findings.** Not every loan or liability will be your problem. Some will be extinguished when the house is auctioned. Some won't. And every lien will have a point in time in which it was recorded.

These three steps allow you to find the potential problems with title, and then sort those that will survive auction in priority sequence.

A. Check for Outstanding Property Taxes

Every homeowner pays taxes to their local government based on the value of their property.

At least, they're *supposed* to. When someone stops paying their mortgage long enough to wind up in foreclosure, there's a solid chance they've stopped paying their property taxes too. That means many of the homes you'll bid on at auction will have back taxes owing. Those taxes will need to be paid by *you* if you successfully buy on the courthouse steps. While some liabilities vanish in foreclosure (keep reading), taxes aren't one of them!

This isn't the end of the world. It's just part of the process. What's important is that you know about any taxes owing so you can add them to your calculations.

Your first job is to find the online home of property tax records for the county you're interested in. Simply search using the name of the county and the words "tax bill." This will usually give you a link to the online portal where you can search and pay for property taxes owing.

Make sure the legal description of the record you're looking at matches the one on your spreadsheet. Each tract of land in a county gets a unique number called an assessor's parcel number, or APN. That number is used to identify a property for things like deeds, taxes, and title information. Records will often include the APN, and it makes for a good unique identifier.

Some counties will ask if you're searching for secured or unsecured property. You want secured property—things like houses and land (note that mobile homes are considered unsecured property).

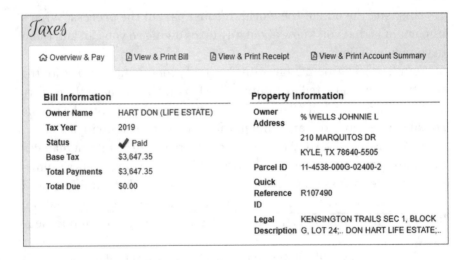

Look for any sign of unpaid taxes. They'll be indicated by phrases like "delinquent tax amount" or "prior year taxes owing."

Note that, in some cases, there are both county taxes *and* city taxes. It's not common, but it does happen—and when it does, they're usually tracked separately. A quick way to check is to search online using the name of the city and the words "tax bill." You can also double-check further by calling the county and city offices.

If you've checked for outstanding taxes and done the rest of the title search that follows and you're confident you want to bid on the property, there's a special line item on the bid sheet from the previous chapter for past-due taxes.

Some states and counties have foreclosure processes for overdue property taxes. When you see that the taxes are several years overdue or there are signs of litigation for overdue taxes or previous tax foreclosures, you'll often need to contact the county to request further information to get the whole story. We often skip such properties altogether.

Now is also a good time to add the annual tax amount to your spreadsheet if you haven't already. If you plan to rent the property or own it for any significant period before flipping it, you'll need the tax amount to properly calculate your expenses.

B. Find the L's: Liens, Lawsuits, and Liabilities

Property taxes are certainly not the only encumbrance on a property. We address them separately because (a) they're easy to find, and (b) they almost always must be paid. Outstanding property taxes tend to be straightforward.

There are other types of liens, however. Here are the most common:

- **First mortgages.** This is the most common type of lien on residential property.
- **Second and third mortgages.** A borrower may turn to these for additional funds to buy or upgrade a home.
- **Judgment liens.** If a homeowner is sued and loses, the winning party may file a lien on the property.
- **HOA and COA liens.** Homeowner and condominium owner associations have the power to register liens too.
- **Mechanic's liens.** Unpaid contractors, tradespeople, and suppliers of materials can register liens.
- **IRS and tax liens.** Unpaid taxes can lead to liens.
- **UCC.** A UCC lien filing, or UCC filing, is a notice lenders file when a personal or a business loan is secured to an asset. It stands for Uniform Commercial code and it survives foreclosure. An example of a UCC would be for a water heater, or water softener—that lien

is attached to the water softener, so if the water softener is gone when you buy the house, you won't have to pay the lien. If the water softener is still there, you will need to pay the lien before selling.

- **Child support and alimony liens.** The same goes for family obligations.

Some liens are *voluntary*, like mortgages—you agree to them when you borrow the money. Some are *involuntary*, like tax and mechanic's liens—they happen without your consent. But they're all very real.

To see how these can stack up, let's go back to poor Dave.

Imagine Dave has a first mortgage balance of $150,000, but he also secured a recent *second* mortgage for $50,000 from a different bank so he could build an addition. That second mortgage holder also registered a lien on the property.

Here's what we have now:

- **First mortgage:** $150,000
- **Second mortgage:** $50,000

However, as part of the renovation, Dave upgraded the HVAC system in his house, which cost $10,000. When Dave didn't pay promptly, the tradesman who did the work placed a mechanic's lien on the property.

Now Dave's situation looks like this:

- **First mortgage:** $150,000
- **Second mortgage:** $50,000
- **Mechanic's lien:** $10,000

But it doesn't end there. (Dave's in a lot of trouble.) Dave also owes taxes to the IRS, and they've placed a lien on his property for $5,000.

- **First mortgage:** $150,000
- **Second mortgage:** $50,000
- **Mechanic's lien:** $10,000
- **IRS lien:** $5,000

When you see Dave's house on a list of properties scheduled for foreclosure, you don't know all this at first glance. You just know *somebody* is foreclosing on a loan that used Dave's house as collateral. That somebody wants their money back, and they're going to sell Dave's house to get it.

As the person who might be interested in buying that house, you need to understand all the possible encumbrances on that property (this step) and then the *survival* and *priority* of those encumbrances (the next step): Which will still exist after foreclosure, and what's their priority? Who gets paid first?

To do that, you need to visit the website of your old friend the county clerk. Do a search by property and by owner name.

Here's what you're looking for:
- Deeds—Changes Owner of Record
- Deeds of trust—Loan on Property
- Subordination agreement
- UCC filing
- Order
- *Lis pendens*
- Tax lien
- Mechanic's lien
- Reconveyance (This is a notice that a loan/lien has been paid off and is no longer valid.)
- Subordination agreement (This is recorded when someone refinances a loan in first position but is keeping an old second loan. It says that, even though the smaller second loan was recorded first, this is in a subordinate position to the more recent loan.)
- Notice of Action (This means there is litigation pending with one of the property owners and it should be looked at closely to see if it affects the property.)
- Notice (This could mean anything; if hundreds of property owners are affected, then it's likely not an issue, but if fewer owners are affected, it may be worth looking at.)
- Assn Lien (HOA liens are likely not an issue.)
- Utility Liens
- FTL or Federal Tax Lien (These do not go away after foreclosure, so the full amount owed must be determined.)
- Request for reconveyance (If this shares the same document number as the deed of trust, it is a hint that the deed of trust is a second lien...and we don't want to buy second liens.)

And really, any other sort of document, too. Be on the lookout for any document you can find for that person and property to see whether there is something strange related to it.

For properties with a long or troubled history, you may see a lot of documents. A loan could have been sold from one party to another. A mortgage could be renewed. A property could be severed or have its description changed.

For each one that you find, you'll want to:

- First, verify that it's for the correct property using APN numbers, legal property descriptions, owner names, and loan numbers—anything that ensures you're looking at the right property.
- Second, list each encumbrance (liens, etc.) *and its filing date* on a separate spreadsheet. Don't skip this part—you'll need it in the next step.

Let's do a sample title search for a property that I own. Remember, we are trying to figure out which loan is in first position, and if there are any extra liens due. Early on, we already checked property taxes, so now we jump right in to record search.

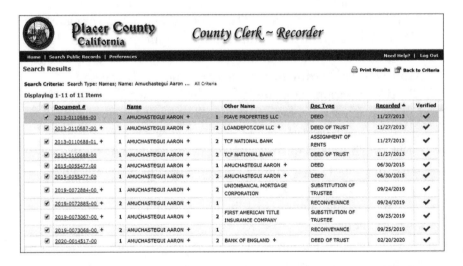

We add all of these into our spreadsheet in the order they were recorded, then we look closer at the documents to see what they say. At first glance, it would look like there are three loans on the property (Deeds of Trust) and that the first position loan is number 0110687 because it was recorded first. You can follow the notes on the title spreadsheet below.

Checklist:

Property Tax Check _Paid_ (Paid or list Unpaid Amount)
Recorded Document Check

Document Type	Name	Doc Number	Amount	Notes
Deed	AAron Amuchastegui	0110686		Aaron Bought Property
Deed of Trust	"	~~0110687~~		① Loan
Assignment of Rents	"	0110688		Misc. Doc - Part of other
Deed of Trust	"	~~0110688~~		② Loan
DEED	"	0055477		Misc Doc - Added a Trust
DEED	"	0055477		"
Subs. Trustee	"	0072884		Defines New trustee for loan
Reconveyance	"	0072885		Says 0110687 is Paid off
Subst Trustee	"	0073067		Defines New trustee
Reconveyance	"	0073068		Says 0110688 is Paid off
Deed of Trust	"	0014517		③ Loan

Grant Deed:
    Check APN Matches ✓
    Check Address Matches ✓
    Check "Computed For Full Value" is checked for non-family transfers ✓
Deed of Trust
    Check Document number matches "Notice of Default" number in our spreadsheet
    Check APN Matches ✓
    Check Address Matches ✓
    Check Addendums for no reference to affordable housing or govt agencies ✓
Notice Of Default
    Check Document number matches First Deed of Trust ____
    Check Trustee Sale Number Matches ____
    Check APN Matches (If applicable, not always on NOD) ____
    Check Address Matches (If applicable, not always on NOD) ____
Notice Of Trustee Sale
    Check Document number matches First Deed of Trust ____
    Check Trustee Sale Number Matches Profile Sheet ____
    Check APN Matches ____
    Check Address Matches ____
    Check Dollar Value Makes Sense (Close to loan value, usually higher) ____

After reading all of the documents we see there is only one upaid loan on the property and there are not any other liens, lawsuits, or issues. Deed of Trust with Document number 00145517 is the 1st position (and is the only loan in this case). If a notice of trustee sale referenced that loan, it would be a safe title. If it referred to any other loan, it would not.

Once you've listed all the encumbrances and their recording date, it's time to sort out which liens matter and how much.

C. Filter and Prioritize Your Findings

You should now have a list of registered documents related to the property, with relevant filing dates.

Your final task is to remove any liens that won't matter after foreclosure and sort the remaining ones in priority order.

1. Remove Any Lien That Won't Survive Foreclosure

Let's check Dave's situation again:

- **First mortgage:** $150,000
- **Second mortgage:** $50,000
- **Mechanic's lien:** $10,000
- **IRS lien:** $5,000

Recall that not all liens are created equal. Some vanish when the house is sold on the courthouse steps. For example, here are the liens that generally do not survive foreclosure, so you don't need to worry about them. (Remember that things do change over time and could vary from state-to-state, so please review your state's law and check out our resource page to see if there are updates to this section at BiggerPockets.com/ForeclosureBonus.)

- HOA/ASM Liens for unpaid HOA fees
- State Tax Liens
- Hospital Liens
- Mechanics Liens (Unless they predate the deed of trust)
- FTL/Federal Tax Liens (They only go away if you wait 120 days, or pay them off before that)

Here is a list of liens that do survive foreclosure. You will need to plan to deal with them either through effort or cost (or both).

- Order (Court order)
- *Lis pendens* (Active lawsuit restricting property rights)
- FTL/Federal Tax Liens (They only go away if you wait 120 days, or pay them off before that)
- Mechanic's lien (If it predates Deed of Trust)
- UCC Liens

In Dave's state, the mechanic's lien will be wiped out after foreclosure.

That's too bad for the contractor but good news for you—you can strike that one off the list.

That leaves just three liens:
- **First mortgage:** $150,000
- **Second mortgage:** $50,000
- **IRS lien:** $5,000

In many cases, a federal tax lien will disappear after 120 days. That's good news in the long run, and you can strike it. In the shorter term, if you want to sell the property, you're either going to have to wait four months or pay off the lien. If you want to bid on this property and flip it immediately, now would be a good time to add this amount to your bid sheet and adjust your maximum bid.

2. Prioritize the Remaining Liens

Let's check Dave's situation again. Let's assume we've added the IRS lien to our bid sheet, so we'll drop it off the list.
- **First mortgage:** $150,000
- **Second mortgage:** $50,000

Dave's case, as tough as it is on Dave, is easy from a title perspective. There are just two major liens. If we check the dates, we can see that the first mortgage was indeed recorded a few years before the second.

Now we can answer one final, critical question:

Which Loan Are You Buying?

You now have a list of foreclosure-surviving liens, sorted by their dates.

Remember that *loans* are foreclosed on, not homes. So when we buy Dave's "house" at auction, we're really purchasing a loan. Our very last task, which will determine whether we want to bid on Dave's house, is to *make sure we're buying the loan at the top of the list.*

Lien priority, or position, determines who gets paid first after a foreclosure sale. The general rule is that—other than property taxes, which almost always remain in first position—loans are prioritized in a "first recorded, first paid" sequence.

Our rule is simple: *We buy only first-position loans.* There are people who buy second-position loans, but we aren't those people.

What if, for example, it was the second mortgage holder who decided to exercise their claim to Dave's property because he hasn't paid them? If you buy *that* loan at auction, some of the ones that come after it will go away. But the first mortgage *won't*. That debt will still be owed. Foreclosure doesn't erase everything.

If you buy Dave's house at auction and it turns out you've bought the loan in second position, then the debt for the first-position loan and its priority lien (the first mortgage), is still there!

To find out, check the foreclosure notice, which will specify the lender and the loan number. Now compare it against your list. Where is it in the sequence?

> **LESSON:** Be sure you understand (a) which loan you're buying, and (b) where it falls in the pecking order.

Subordination Agreements

As you prowl the list of recorded documents for your property, you may see *subordination agreements*. They play an important role in getting your list of encumbrances in the correct order.

Imagine you take a first mortgage to buy a home, then take a second mortgage to do a renovation—just like Dave. A few years later, you're still paying off both mortgages, but your first is due for renewal.

When you renew your first, technically it is a new mortgage and now falls behind the second mortgage in the pecking order. Banks don't like that, so a subordination agreement is used to legally say, "Hey, even though this loan happened after that other one, this is really the one that's in front."

Make sure you review any subordination agreements to be certain you get your list in the right sequence.

Lien Survival versus Loan Survival

Foreclosure eliminates a number of liens in most states. But it certainly doesn't eliminate all debt. So although the *lien* may disappear, the *loan* may not, which does create the possibility that someone could still come after you as the new owner. Your best recourse here is to go to an expert for advice.

Title Déjà Vu

By now, you've likely noticed that during the five steps, you keep revisiting resources you've been to before. You might be asking, *Why didn't I get this information while I was at the recorder's office last time?*

Remember that the purpose of each of the five steps in our process is to narrow down the number of properties you're considering *at each step*. Yes, you could have gathered title-relevant information while you were on the county clerk's website in Step 1, but you would have had to review the documents for dozens of properties, many of which would have never made it through your filter. Why dig for title details on a property you don't have the budget for? Why pull the property tax records for a place that doesn't fit your skill set?

It's a lot faster to revisit a property in order to dig a little deeper than it is to dig deeper on a long list of properties that are never going to make the cut.

Disclaimer: Go to the Pros

Title research can be complicated and time-consuming. But it's also non-negotiable—it *has* to happen if you want to manage your risk at auction.

I have two pieces of advice. The first is to know that you will get faster and better at it. Just like everything else, it simply takes a little time and effort. What starts as a struggle with an overwhelming list of documents in legalese soon becomes a quick and effortless task.

That being said, it's wise to consider professional help when you're starting out. Consult a lawyer who specializes in real estate law and title or find a title company that will do foreclosure title work. It's the best way to check your work and protect your investment. When you're new to title research, the double-coverage approach can be very worthwhile.

Title Research Pays Off

Remember the first property we bought at auction? Not only was I panicking about handing all my money to someone who arrived by skateboard, but I was deeply unsettled by the fact that I was the only person bidding. No one seemed to want to touch the property during the auction. That, more than anything, made me worry that I'd made a horrible mistake.

Once we had a few auctions under our belt, however, I realized just why we'd had no competition at auction and got a great price as a result.

At the time, the company providing foreclosure listings in the area had included the property on their list, but they indicated it was a second deed of trust that was being foreclosed on. That would have meant we'd be buying a loan in second position, which is not something we want to do.

However, in doing my homework, I'd found the subordination agreement that showed the loan in default—the one we'd be buying—was actually in *first* position. Even though it wasn't the first loan by calendar date, it had been moved into first position by the subordination agreement.

Had I not done the title research and been thorough about it, I would likely never have even shown up at auction. Instead, the extra legwork not only showed that this was a worthwhile property to bid on, but it gave me an advantage over the other bidders.

The thorough title review not only kept us safe—it gave us an edge!

It's Time to Get Ready for Auction!

Let's review where we are in the five-step process. So far, we've completed the first four steps:

- **Step 1:** Create or purchase a list of properties slated for auction.
- **Step 2:** Drive by those of interest to learn more.
- **Step 3:** Analyze the remaining desired properties to come up with a bid price.
- **Step 4:** Do a title review of any property you plan to bid on.

If you've worked through these steps with a list of real properties, you'll notice that with each step, you're narrowing your list of potential properties, effectively focusing on those that fit your unique interests, skills, risk tolerance, and budget.

Title review is the last step before the final, exciting step of going to the auction. Any property that still remains on your list is likely to be something you'll at least hope to bid on.

Up to this point, you may have done much of the legwork on your own, with only limited contact with other people. Now it's time to dive right into auction day, when all your hard work can pay off!

CHAPTER 8
STEP 5:
THE AUCTION

Deconstructing a Day on the Courthouse Steps

After we'd been in the auction game for a while, it became even more apparent just how important it was to have as many opportunities as possible to bid. The more we could bid, the greater our chance of success. We were determined to become good fishermen.

In our area, however, auctions would often happen in different locations on the same day. To increase our odds of success, one of my partners would attend one auction and I'd attend another.

On one such double-auction day, I was headed from Sacramento toward an auction in the Bay Area. From my research, I knew there were several appealing properties on the docket.

Depending on attendance, I knew I could do well, but I was bouncing up against another limiting factor. Not only were we constrained by how many auctions we could attend, but we simply didn't have an unlimited supply of cash. Paying in cashier's checks meant we couldn't just buy properties like crazy and then sort out the financing after. It was cash on the barrelhead, and we only had so much to go around.

I was mentally reviewing some of my top picks for the day when my phone rang. Bad news: My partner had been unsuccessful at his auction and was headed home.

I was disappointed. Here I was, headed to a virtual property bonanza, and I'd be limited by how much I could buy. Meanwhile, my partner would be sitting at home with a stack of money that I couldn't access and he couldn't spend.

I pictured him driving north along the freeway and the two of us passing each other like ships in the night, him with cash, me with opportunity. Both of us missing our chance.

Then it hit me. *He was driving on the freeway.* I began doing the mental math. My auction was supposed to start in an hour. Time was tight. *Could it work?*

I got back on the phone.

Minutes later, I caught sight of his car up ahead. He'd turned around and was now in the right-hand lane, traveling as slowly as he could safely get away with, while I was in the passing lane, driving as *fast* as I could safely get away with.

He pulled onto the shoulder. I stopped behind him and sprinted toward his car. His arm shot out the window, and a white envelope flapped in the breeze. I grabbed it, turned on my heels like an NFL receiver, and began running back toward my car. Over the noise of the traffic, I heard him yell, "GO!"

Ten seconds later I was back on the freeway, accelerating toward the Bay Area with six figures' worth of extra checks on the seat beside me.

The auction was scheduled to start at 1 p.m. I pulled into the location with minutes to spare, then began frantically driving in circles trying to find a spot in the public lot. Finally, I spied something that, while not technically a legal parking space, was just big enough to fit my car. I squeezed in and slammed the car into park. I had one minute to spare.

Jumping out, I sprinted across the lot and over to the courthouse, with my envelopes and paperwork crumpled in my fist. As the municipal clock struck one, I skidded into the courthouse steps, doubled over and heaving for breath.

As I recovered, I heard a voice call out a property address. I looked up to find a trustee in front of me holding a clipboard.

I looked around. I was the only other person there.

Still gasping for air, I bid a penny over the starting bid and bought a great property using our combined cashier's checks.

Moments later, I was filling out paperwork as two other bidders came around the corner. They were interested in the property I'd just bought.

I looked at my watch. They'd missed their chance by less than five minutes.

This, at its heart, is the essence of buying properties at auction: The deals are out there, but they almost always go to people who are willing to go the extra mile.

The truth was, it wasn't *that* hard to pull over on the freeway and grab an envelope and then sprint across a parking lot. But that little extra effort ensured that I not only arrived on time but had the additional cash to make a much larger investment.

Putting in that extra effort—deciding to reshuffle plans on the fly and make it work—was about *mindset.* It would have been easier to pull off the freeway and meet at a gas station or a coffee shop, but we would have missed our shot at an empty courthouse *and* an investment that turned out to be almost twice as profitable as it would have been if we'd had to compete with other bidders.

The Foreclosure Auction Mindset

Auction success, then, is fundamentally a mindset. The people who do well aren't just those who are good with spreadsheets, or know how to swing a hammer, or have extra cash. They're people who understand how to think about the job at hand in a way that other people can't or won't.

Successful auction buyers see things differently. They know, for example, that:

- **Problems mean opportunities.** Every problem you solve—whether that's figuring out whether a property is occupied or jumping out on the freeway to grab cash from your partner—is something you can be rewarded for.
- **Challenges keep other people away.** Those same problems you're willing to face are problems that other people won't. They don't have your resolve or your grit. Those are the people who *don't* go to auction. Or the ones who show up two minutes late after you just bid a penny over.
- **Risk means reward.** Solving problems creates opportunities. The auction mindset is about *falling in love with the problems.* That may sound crazy, but let it sink in: The problems, the risks, the unknowns—that's where the opportunity is. As with everything else in life, the spoils go the winner. And when it comes to auctions, the winner is the person who falls in love with—and as a result, *solves*—the most problems.

Developing that mindset takes time and experience. That experience begins with attending your first auction—just as an observer if you like—and soaking up the surreal experience that awaits.

The Auction Experience

We've seen auctions happen in some odd places—hotels, offices, or even at the home being sold. This is more often the case with judicial foreclosures, where, after due process, a judge has authorized the sale of a property.

At least 90 percent of the time, though, foreclosed homes are sold at the courthouse. Two things are surprising to most people when they attend their first auction.

The first is how casual it can be—not casual in the sense of slow-paced (things can happen very quickly) but in the sense of ad hoc. There are people simply standing around everywhere. It can be hard to tell the bidders from the criers. One trustee might be wearing a suit; another might be wearing shorts and a T-shirt. And because everything is happening outside in a public space, you can walk amid all of it. An auction feels more like a spontaneous farmers' market than ground zero for millions of dollars in real estate transactions.

The second is how quickly things can transition from casual to confusing and chaotic. There can be multiple criers. There might be five or six different trustees auctioning houses at the same time, all within a few feet of each other. There are people milling about everywhere. Cars might be roaring past on the street, and it can get hard to hear. There are numbers and addresses being called out and people muttering and shuffling through paperwork.

If you've ever been to a casino and tried to figure out a game you've never played, you have a sense of what it's like. Walk up to a craps table in Vegas, and you'll see a crowd of people shouting, money being passed around, chips being stacked, bets being placed, and the first time you go, *none* of it will make any sense. You'll feel like you're not even speaking the same language.

That's what a first auction is like.

Yet somehow, there's order in the chaos, and there's a formal structure beneath the casual surface. Here's what the process looks like.

1. Hurry Up and Wait

Every auction has a start time, but that doesn't mean any bidding is going to happen right away. Often, there's a kind of "hurry up and wait" scenario—everyone is standing around waiting for something to happen. While many bidders will show up on time or early, trustees can be much less predictable. Don't be surprised if they arrive later than the start time.

You'll notice that many attendees know each other—like us, they've been to many auctions, and eventually you get to know the players. To pass the time, there's conversation—small talk, mainly. Although a kind of camaraderie develops over time, the other bidders are still your competition, so most people aren't talking about specifics of that day's bids.

It can be boring. It can be cold. Or hot. Or wet. But you need to wait it out. The minute you leave to use the restroom could be the minute a trustee starts selling.

2. The Trustees/Auctioneers Appear

Out of this expectant atmosphere, a trustee—or several—will emerge and begin selling. Just like that. In an instant, people go from casually chatting to rushing up to the trustee.

Most bidders have some kind of information with them. They may have a phone or tablet where they can check their bids and their records and update their files. Other people are holding laptops, ready to research on the fly. Some people are holding clipboards. Others don't seem to be holding anything, but if you look closely, you'll see they're wearing an earpiece and communicating with someone else in real time.

Before the bidding begins, the trustee has some legal obligations. For each property, they will announce they are taking the property to auction. They'll list the owner's name, the lender (usually a bank), and the date of the mortgage. Not only is this a legal requirement, but it also helps the bidders orient themselves. If you're bidding on several places, you'll be able to check your listing to see whether the details the trustee announces fit yours. It's a final check to make sure you're bidding on the right place or, more accurately, the right *loan*.

Most trustees are attorneys, not professional auctioneers. They don't speak in the high-speed chants you'd hear at more traditional auctions. They may be dressed in suits, or they may be as casual as our man on the skateboard.

Some events also use professional auctioneers. The pros are usually easier to find—they may have bright shirts or banners to identify themselves, and they tend to have the polished auctioneer style. They're usually representing multiple banks/lenders or other trustees.

In either case, they'll announce the process and then open the bidding.

3. The Bidding Begins

Things kick off with the trustee declaring the opening bid. The lender can decide this amount—from as low as a dollar to as high as what's owed on the property plus legal fees. They usually can't choose to set the opening bid any higher than that, but any lower starting point is fair game.

Once the opening bid is stated, the trustee can accept bids. The property then sells for the highest one. If a property doesn't sell, the title reverts to the beneficiary—typically the bank that provided the mortgage. From there, it will usually end up as an REO (real estate owned) property, as discussed earlier.

The bidding process is similar to any other auction. As people begin to bid, they yell out numbers back and forth.

The trustee might say, "Okay, opening bid is $100,000."

Someone will call out 101, and the trustee will say, "Okay, I have a $101,000 bid from John. Anyone else?"

Someone else calls out 102, and the trustee responds, "Okay, I have a $102,000 bid from Anna."

The process goes onward from there. There may be five or ten bidders, or there could be just two. And they'll go back and forth for a while until they reach a point where the bids have stopped increasing.

"Now it's $115,000 with John," the trustee says. He looks around at the bidders. Everybody's shaking their head no.

And just like on TV, the trustee says, "Going once, going twice, sold."

Professional auctioneers will often drag the whole process out longer than a trustee will. Pros often have a bit more of a pitch. "Are you sure no one wants this?" an auctioneer might ask. "This is a great house—three bedrooms, two baths." They'll wait as long as it takes for people to make a decision.

The difference in style has to do with incentives. A professional auctioneer may be getting paid a percentage, while a trustee just needs to get the job done and move on to the next auction. The faster they can wrap things up, the sooner they get to go home.

The exception is that sometimes a trustee may be waiting on

confirmation to sell a property. They may announce, "I'm ready to sell 145 Main Street, but we'll be waiting on 216 Central Avenue." The reason is that someone, somewhere is trying to put together a deal or a delay to keep the foreclosure from going forward. At some point, that trustee will get a call confirming whether to go ahead with the property, delay it, or cancel it.

4. Paperwork and Money

Once the bidding has ended and the trustee has declared the property sold, they'll ask the winning bidder to hand over their cashier's checks. At that point, they may pause the auction to confirm payment, or they may try to keep moving and get through their list. Either way, they'll have to stop at some point to verify that each successful bidder has the money, and then issue receipts.

If you're the successful bidder, you'll need to stick around to get your receipt, verify the details on it, and take a photo of the paperwork (more on this, and what follows, in Chapter 10).

If you're *not* the successful bidder, you may want to stick around anyway. It doesn't happen often, but sometimes bidders don't actually have the proper funds, or they may even change their mind before handing over the cash. In those cases, the property is re-auctioned, with that bidder excluded.

Solving the Paradox of Auction

All told, auctions are oddly bipolar events. They're both simple and complex, casual yet chaotic. To complicate things further, no two auctions are exactly alike.

Luckily, however, auctions are *free and open to the public*. That means you can simply show up and watch! It's the best foreclosure education you can get.

Make a point of attending an auction simply to observe. It costs nothing but time, and you'll learn more in an hour of watching an auction than you will in days of reading. Grab a coffee and enjoy the action.

Preparing for Auction

Over the years, we've developed an approach to auctions that works for us, and that we now teach to others who bid on our behalf.

1. Take It Seriously

Although many people go into the auction process thinking they're taking it seriously, in my experience, people often don't take the process seriously *enough*.

Part of this is simply the marathon leading up to auction. You've been building lists, analyzing properties, driving by addresses, and getting financially prepared. You may have met with Realtors, attorneys, bankers, partners, and contractors. That's a lot, so you may be tempted to treat the auction as the easy home stretch.

Don't let up just yet. Push the extra mile. Auction day is the culmination of all that hard work, and it's worthwhile to stay focused. Therefore:

- **Be early.** Trustees are notoriously unreliable when it comes to start times. After a while, you can get complacent and start arriving late, since "things never really get started until 9:30." But that's exactly when the trustee will be right on time and sell the property you wanted while you're still looking for a parking spot. Just come a little early.
- **Dress right.** Auctions happen rain or shine, hot or cold, and they happen outside a great deal. Come prepared and you'll avoid getting frostbitten, sunburned, or drenched. Dress appropriately.
- **Pack food and drink.** It's not *that* much of a marathon, but if you think your thirst or blood sugar might cause you to lose focus or wander away in search of street food, you'd better pack a few snacks.
- **Prepare for the long haul.** Use the restroom *before* things start to happen. Losing a house because you had to slip off for a quick break is no fun for you, and even less fun to explain to your partners.

2. Prepare Your Bid Sheet

As we'll see in the next chapter, the strange world of auctions has a way of making people behave strangely, too. It's easy to lose control of your rational mind and get caught up in the excitement of millions of dollars changing hands in a competitive atmosphere.

For now, understand that one of your best tools for staying rational on auction day is to carefully *plan your maximum bids in advance.*

By the end of Step 4, you should have come up with a bid sheet for each property you plan to bid on. It should, at the very bottom, have one magic number: the most you should pay for the property in order to turn a profit.

There are two ways to approach the bid sheets. You can bring one for each property—that's the easiest approach if you are bidding on a limited number of houses.

Alternatively, you can create a one-page list that has all the relevant information you'll need in the heat of the moment—including the all-important maximum bid.

Bid Amt	ID	Borrower	Address	Legal Description	Value($)	City Code
BASS, ROBERT ALEX (10-1)						
$104,000	33	HARDISON, YOMI	4600 CAUSEWAY CT	LOT: 0038 BLOCK: 007 Subdivision: THE BRIDGEWOOD ADDITION PHASE:	$138,000	KILLEEN
KEMP, JUSTIN (10-1)						
$226,000	35	MENDEZ, ROGELIO	485 SPRINGS VALLEY LN	A8860BC L WALKER, 53-7, ACRES 4.78 53-7.	$365,322	BELTON
LATHAM, JOHN (10-1)						
$24,000	29	ALFORD, JAMES	2950 BRIGGS RD	L-9.1 FLORENCE HILLS ESTATES	$59,699	KILLEEN
$128,000	27	ANTHONY/ZINA, HOOD	5500 HUNTERS RIDGE TRL	L-30 9 TIMBER RIDGE ESTATES 2	$175,924	KILLEEN
$129,000	17	CURRIE, KARLA	4303 CAPRI DR	DIAMOND HILLS ADDITION, BLOCK 005, LOT 0007	$136,852	KILLEEN
Pass	2	DREW, GARY/TRACI	146 JESSE JAMES DR	TUMBLEWEED ESTATES, BLOCK 306, LOT 0005, ACRES .500	$262,092	NOLANVILLE
124,000	15	HAWKINS, ROY/RUBY	2620 SNOW BIRD DR	SKIPCHA MOUNTAIN ESTATES PHASE TWENTY THREE, BLOCK 061, LOT 0012	$189,510	HARKER HEIGHTS
RASNER, BLAKE (10-1)						
Pass Bad title	16	DORN, ROBERT	512 NECHES ST	LOT: 4 BLOCK: 1 Subdivision: RIVER PLACE ADDITION SECTION ONE PHASE:	$116,271	BELTON
Pass - Fire	34	NORMAN, CHRISTOPHER/ALISHA	0 MOUNTAIN CREEK RD	A07260C M READ, TRACT 73 MOUNTAIN CREEK RANCH, ACRES 8.63 TRACT 73 MOUNTAIN CREEK RANCH,	$78,469	BELL COUNTY RURAL
	27	SPARKMAN, KEVIN/SHANAN	7289 FM 1570		$500	SALADO

This sheet can save the day at auction, but only if you fill it out in advance. Do it the day before and make any necessary notes on it that you might need.

As they say in the gambling world: Know your limit and play within it.

3. Get Your Checks

Auctions are a cash business. With rare exceptions, if you successfully buy a house at auction, you'll need to pay for it right there. Some auctions will allow a couple of days for winners to come up with the cash, but more often or not, the trustee will ask to see your payment right on the spot. In fact, the trustee will often stop the auction to verify your funds, like someone checking your bingo card to make sure you really do have everything you say.

Cash, however, doesn't mean an actual suitcase of bills. It generally means a cashier's check. Auction officials like them because *they're drawn against the bank's funds, not yours.* You purchase the cashier's check from the bank using the cash in your account. The bank takes your money, and then *they* issue a check.

A certified check is similar, but the funds are actually drawn against the money in *your* account—*you* issue the check. The bank is simply verifying that the funds are there, and signing the check or marking it as official, certified, or accepted in some way.

To buy at auction, then, you're going to need cashier's checks. But because you don't know how much the property is going to cost, you have to bring as much as you're willing and able to spend.

Fortunately, you don't need exact change—the trustee will issue you a check later with the difference. That, however, can take time. And during that time, your money is tied up.

Your objective, then, is to pay an amount *as close as possible* to the price of the house. To do that, you'll need multiple checks.

Let's say you want to buy a house at auction and your maximum bid is $150,000. That's also all the money you have. You bring a cashier's check to auction for $150,000, but you get lucky: You're able to purchase the property for $120,000!

The good news is that you'll get to buy the property—just hand over your check and all is well.

The bad news is that the check with your refund—the $30,000 of "change" you have due back from the transaction—is going to take weeks to arrive from the trustee. Those are weeks when you can't use that money. You can't go to other auctions with it or use it to renovate the property you just bought. It's simply tied up; it's not earning interest for you, and in fact, you may be *paying* interest on it if you borrowed the money.

The solution to this dilemma is to bring multiple cashier's checks of different amounts, so that you can get as close as possible to the selling price while minimizing your refund. At the same time, however, you also want to minimize the total number of checks, because the bank charges you a fee for each one, and dealing with fifty cashier's checks is time-consuming.

So how do you decide how many checks to bring and in what amounts? Easy:

- Bring one check for the *minimum* amount you think you'll pay. If you're looking at a house with a $100,000 maximum bid but you think you *might* get it for as low as $75,000, bring a check for the lower amount.

- Bring smaller-denomination checks that allow you to build up to your maximum bid. In the previous example, you might bring a check for $75,000, two for $10,000, and one for $5,000. You'll have enough to go up to your $100,000 limit, plus the flexibility to pay in increments without leaving too much extra for the trustee.

Once you have your checks, inventory them all on a single sheet where you can see each check, its amount, and the check number. Take photos of the individual checks, too.

Check Number	Bank	Amount
1214568	Wells Fargo	$5,000
1214569	Wells Fargo	$10,000
1214570	Wells Fargo	$10,000
1214571	Wells Fargo	$30,000
1214572	Wells Fargo	$55,000
1214573	Wells Fargo	$80,000
1214574	Wells Fargo	$100,000
1214575	Wells Fargo	$100,000
1214576	Wells Fargo	$200,000
49062	Bank of America	$75,000

4. Auction Day Checklist

You shouldn't need everything on this list. After all, going to an auction isn't a military expedition. But the following checklist might just be your key to success on auction day.

- Identification
- Cashier's checks
- Check inventory
- Pen
- Final bid list
- Snacks and water
- Hat, jacket, etc.
- Umbrella
- Cell phone
- Clipboard

- Laptop or tablet (optional)
- Extra phone battery, if possible
- Headphones
- Pre-made labels with vesting information
- Tax ID for buyer

To Bid or Not to Bid

As with the rest of the steps in our process, you don't *have* to handle this yourself. We use bidders who go to auction on our behalf, with strict instructions on what to buy and how much to bid. It's a fishing technique—we need to be at as many auctions as possible in order to maximize our chances. You can send someone to bid on your behalf, too.

Alternatively, you could use one of the companies that are starting to spring up that offer auction bidding as a service to investors. Naturally, they charge for the service, which reduces your profit, but it's another legitimate way to buy.

When you're starting out, of course, you can just go yourself. You may only have the resources to buy one property, and that's fine. It's your choice to make. You bid what you want, for what you want. Just remember that auctions are fluid events. Trustees and other officials don't always show up on time. Things don't always go according to schedule. Sometimes, there's a lot of hurry up and wait. When you've been standing around for two hours, it can be tempting to slip off to your car, or the restroom, or a nearby café.

But although auctions can start late, they can also start *quickly*. You might run to the restroom only to come back five minutes later and discover that the trustee has arrived, and a handful of properties have already sold.

Arrive at the auction prepared to go the extra mile. Dress right. Hit the restroom before the start time. Pack snacks and a bottle of water. Wear a hat. Bring an umbrella if the weather looks rough. Do what it takes to arrive on time and stick it out.

Listen carefully. It's not impossible for there to be two borrowers with the same name or two houses on the same street. Stay focused and follow your bid sheet.

Onward to Part III

Congratulations! You've just completed the last of our five steps—the exact process we've used to buy millions of dollars' worth of foreclosed real estate. In our experience, following these five steps is a reliable way to find foreclosed properties, buy them on the courthouse steps, and make a profit doing it!

However, despite all this careful preparation, even experienced bidders can struggle with some of the finer points of auction. In Part III, we're going to look at some of the most common challenges in the foreclosure business, including:

- Managing your thoughts and emotions amid the stress and excitement of auction
- The exact steps to take *after* you buy
- How to find the money to buy at auction when you don't have any
- How to take your very first risk-free steps toward the auction experience

Onward!

BIDDING TO BUY

PART III
NEXT STEPS AND ADVANCED MOVES

CHAPTER 9
BEHAVIORAL AUCTIONOMICS
Bringing Your Best Mental Game to the Courthouse Steps

It was 2009, and my partner and I were driving to our first auction ever—the same one where, in a decision that would haunt me for weeks, I would hand all our investment capital to a kid on a skateboard.

The car that morning was filled with a sense of nervous excitement. We were over-caffeinated, stealing jittery glances at the manila envelope on the dash between us. Inside was all our savings, nicely packaged up in a series of cashier's checks. *It's all there,* I thought. *One little envelope.*

As we drove, we talked through endless scenarios, trying to imagine how things would go. How we *hoped* things would go.

"I hope someone else bids first," my partner said.

"Why?" I asked.

"So then we'll know it's a place worth bidding on."

"That's crazy," I said. "I hope *no one* else bids. Then we won't have competition and we can get a better deal."

There was a moment of silence; then we looked at each other and broke out laughing. We had entirely different perspectives on the best-case scenario, and yet, we were both right. If many people bid on a foreclosure, it probably *is* a less-risky proposition. After all, that's why everyone is bidding.

At the same time, all those extra bidders tend to drive up the price, which then makes the property...riskier!

We were both right, and both wrong. Both nervous, and both not quite thinking clearly. Getting caught up in the emotions of the experience had given us a kind of tunnel vision so that we each could only see things one way.

Now, with hundreds of auctions behind me, I know this is normal. Moreover, it's understandable; auctions are full of uncertainty. Our freshman auction was unpredictable, and yours will be too. It's no different from anything else new and a little risky that you try—the uneasy feeling is a sign that you're stretching yourself.

But while that stretching is the very thing that leads to growth, it can also lead to a host of new problems when you enter the courthouse arena and face the other foreclosure gladiators. In the heat of the moment, things can often go in ways you would never have expected.

From Uncertain to Surreal

Look around a typical auction and you'll see people from all walks of life. There are the professionals—people who have bought hundreds of homes on the courthouse steps. This is their job, their business, their life. Then there are the nonprofessionals—people who are trying to buy their first investment home or maybe even the home they hope to live in one day.

All these people are mixed together. Some will be talking on cell phones, maybe to the person they're bidding for: a boss, a partner, a spouse. Others will be sitting quietly. Some will be bouncing nervously on their toes.

And in their collective pockets are *millions* of dollars.

Some of that money will be handed to a trustee in a suit. Some will be handed to a guy on a skateboard. Some won't be spent at all and will be carried right back home again. And some will be used to compete directly with *you* in an attempt to buy the same property you want.

The whole scene is, in many ways, bizarre. Auctions, it turns out, aren't just uncertain; they're also more than a little surreal.

That combination is a tricky one, and it can make people behave in ways they might not expect or that don't serve them well. Things like competition, uncertainty, novelty, and stress have a way of hijacking your rational brain and letting your emotions take control.

I've seen people get so caught up in the emotion of an auction that they end up bidding more than *double* the amount they felt was safe. That's a sure-fire way to never turn a profit or to take a very long time to do so.

At the other end of the spectrum, I've seen people attend auction after auction and never even bid. They spend hours, days, *weeks* analyzing properties and doing drive-bys. They line up the financing, arrange the checks, prepare their bid sheets. They're beyond ready. Yet when the auction arrives, they sit on the sidelines, too frozen with fear to bid.

But there's no way around it. If you want to buy, you have to bid. Yet the uncertain, emotional experience of auctions creates a perfect storm for losing rational control.

And when you lose control, your money tends to follow.

There are two ways to mitigate this. The first is to attend a lot of auctions and buy a lot of foreclosures. Experience has a wonderful way of creating the wisdom you need to keep your head in the heat of things.

However, saying you need to get good at buying foreclosures so you can be good at buying foreclosures isn't terribly helpful when you're starting out.

Instead, you can use the second approach to keeping your cool: Use a few simple rules and strategies to stay in control on auction day and keep your more primitive brain from going off the rails.

We call this *behavioral auctionomics*. It's about knowing your brain and using that knowledge to your advantage.

Tilt!

As you sit in the comfort of your home with your spreadsheets and your plans, it's easy to think that you won't succumb to any of the typical auction pitfalls. *Of course* you'll keep your cool. *Of course* you'll be rational.

That, of course, is just another pitfall.

The excitement of auction is a different experience from being at home. The competition, the stakes, the excitement, the emotion—they combine in ways that can make you do things you'd *never* do in most situations.

Poker players have a term for this: *tilt*. In poker, it's usually applied when a player's emotions start to negatively affect their play, and it's a great descriptor for what can happen to you at auction. Your emotions—positive or negative—start to get the best of you. You bid on things you shouldn't, or you bid more than you should. In essence, you lose control. Tilting is like having a complete stranger take over your brain while you stand by and watch helplessly.

The aim at auction, then, is to avoid tilt at all costs. To do that, we've outlined our best auction-tested strategies for keeping your cool at the courthouse.

1. Have the Right Goal

One of the effects that auction day has on your brain is that you become more competitive.

It's exhilarating to bid in real time against someone else. Auctions aren't like a chess game. You don't get to sit there and ponder your next move for ten minutes; you need to act quickly. It's less like chess and more like tennis.

In tennis, of course, you really *do* want to beat the other person. At auctions, the primary goal is a little different: You want to buy a house, not beat a person. Yes, beating the competition may be part of the journey. Just remember that you set out to do one thing: acquire a suitable property at an attractive price. What *shouldn't* be on your to-do list is beating someone.

There's nothing wrong with a little friendly competition, and when you begin to know some of the other players who turn up regularly at auction, it can even be a fun part of the camaraderie.

It's *not* helpful, however, when it changes your goal.

> **LESSON:** Your objective is to buy a property at an attractive price, not to win at all costs.

2. Know Your Bid in Advance

The first four steps of our process are designed to do two things very well: identify properties that are a fit for you to bid on, and determine a price for them. Note that the steps are also designed *to be completed in advance.* Keeping your head on straight at auction means making as many decisions as possible before the actual event. For all your good intentions, it can be difficult to stay rational in the heat of the moment, so the more decisions you can make from the comfort of your home, with no competition and the luxury of time to think, the better.

If you've done your job correctly, prior to auction day you'll have a bid sheet prepared with notes and information on the properties that are a fit for you and your budget. Each one will have a maximum bid amount.

Do not exceed that bid. Especially when you're new to auctions.

You will *absolutely* be tempted to. It's almost impossible not to get excited about some of the properties—in fact, it's normal, and we *want* to be excited. Why do it otherwise? But we don't want that excitement to lead us into financial loss.

Your maximum bid price is like a big red STOP sign. It's the limit.

> **LESSON:** Prepare your bids in advance and do not exceed them.

3. Arrive Early and Prepared

We've learned through painful experience that exuberance tends to breed exuberance. Things escalate more when you start from an escalated state.

If you show up late, hungry, and ill-prepared for auction, you're already frazzled. You're like a time bomb of bad decisions just waiting to go off.

So be prepared. Complete the last of your bid sheet work the day before. Pick up your checks the day before. Arrive at auction early. Use the washroom. Bring a jacket, a hat, a drink.

Preparation helps you keep your cool. By controlling as many things as you can, you'll stand a better chance of keeping a leash on the things you can't.

> **LESSON:** Keep your brain and body calm by preparing and arriving early.

4. Listen Carefully

Auctions can be chaotic, noisy, and full of distractions. Focus on the trustee and *listen carefully*. You need to hear the loan and property description clearly. There are a lot of Smiths in the world—there can easily be two of them being foreclosed on at the same time. Cedar Street sounds a lot like Cedar Avenue.

> **LESSON:** Focus and listen carefully—mistakes happen!

5. Don't Bid on Unknown or Discarded Properties

There are likely to be many properties announced at your auction. Unless those houses are on your list and with a bid price that you've established in advance, *they are not for you.*

You'd be surprised at the ways in which a property you haven't analyzed or have already discarded might captivate your more primitive brain. I've experienced each of the following scenarios at auction:

A super-low price.

You might hear a starting bid that seems incredibly cheap. *That's such a bargain,* you tell yourself. *The details really don't matter. I can't lose.* Minutes later, you're at the tail end of a bidding war for something you never intended to buy in the first place.

No one else bids.

Imagine the trustee announces a property with a super-low starting bid. It's not on your list, but no one else is bidding. *Oh my gosh,* you think. *I could buy this place for a song!* And so, even though you know next to nothing about the place, you call out a bid.

What happens next? Someone else thinks, *Huh. Maybe that property IS worth bidding on.* Before you know it, you're in a bidding war and determined to beat out that evil stranger who's trying to buy *your* house (that you've never seen and know nothing about).

You recognize a property that you discarded.

Imagine you start your process with a list of a hundred properties. Along the way, as you work through the steps, you begin to narrow that list. Some properties you discard easily and early. You forget them just as quickly.

Others, however, will make your shortlist. They may even be favorites right up until the title review. Those are the ones you often will remember—especially when the trustee calls out the address.

I remember 786 Pine Street, you think. *Man—that was a great property.*

Suddenly, you're paying attention a little more closely. *Say, that opening bid is really low! Maybe I should jump in.*

Ten minutes later, you're the not-so-proud owner of a property you'd already decided wasn't suitable. *Oops.*

Expect addresses you recognize to be announced at auction. Don't expect to change your mind and start bidding on them in a shopaholic haze.

> **LESSON:** Stick to the properties listed on your bid sheet!

6. Bring a Voice of Reason

Many bidders bring other people with them to auction. For some, this is a fishing strategy. With so many trustees calling out properties, it's easy to miss your shot at a busy auction—while you're bidding on one property, another one on your list could be selling thirty feet away. Many buyers work in small teams so they can cover all the trustees.

When you're new, however, there's an even better reason to bring someone along: to act as your second brain. Give them your properties and your bids. Arrange in advance for them to let you know if you're starting to *tilt*.

> **LESSON:** Bring a friend or partner to auction. It's more fun and it's good for your brain!

7. Accept Going Home Empty-Handed

Last month, we bought a home at auction for thousands of dollars over the maximum bid we'd established the day before. The reason? Our bidders didn't want to go home empty-handed.

It's an easy mistake to make. Auction day requires a lot of preparation, and it's painful to think you might go home with nothing.

Trust me: It's better to go home empty-handed. You can't make money by losing money. And even if you don't buy, you're still going home with an education.

> **LESSON:** Accept in advance that you might not make a purchase.

8. Trust Yourself and the Process

There have been times where I've been swept up in the bidding because I assumed that the other bidders knew more than me. When you're just learning the ropes, it's an easy trap to fall into.

Don't. In the heat of the moment, *trust the work*. If you've followed the process, then you've done the work. Stare single-mindedly at your bid sheet and follow your own instructions.

Think of the bid sheet as a message from your cool and collected past self, sent forward to the anxious, overexcited, present *you* who is standing on the steps.

That person from the day before? That's the one you want to trust.

> **LESSON:** Ignore your feelings about other bidders; trust yourself and the process.

9. Don't Worry About Bidding Style

Auctions have more in common with poker than just tilt. Buyers will often try to be strategic with the style of their bidding. They'll bid a big amount, going all in to scare off competition, or bid a small amount to appear uninterested.

Like poker, it's mostly just bluffing.

In reality, the *style* of bidding doesn't tell you as much as you'd think. It's a tactic that plays to your primitive brain. You can't tell if the "all-in" man in the hat is desperate, bluffing, or just new to auctions. You can't tell if the nervous woman in the jacket is reluctant, broke, or just introverted.

Your best approach is to *focus on the numbers*. Use your bid sheet. All that matters is whether the current bidding is above or below your max bid. If it helps, pick a price increment you can fall back on when you're unsure. You might, for example, make a rule that if you're not sure how much more to bid, bid just $50 more.

As you gain experience, you'll begin to know some of the other players. You can experiment with your own bidding style and follow the style of others. But at first? Just play the numbers. Keep your eye on your own wallet, not anyone else's.

> **LESSON:** Ignore the posturing of other bidders and focus on the numbers.

Money, Money, Everywhere

It's odd to stand in a crowd and know that around you are tens or even hundreds of millions of dollars stuffed into envelopes and pockets. The only time most people get so close to that kind of money is in a bank, where it's in an enormous vault watched by cameras and armed guards.

That's part of the excitement of auction. It's an experience like no other.

I've found it helpful to enjoy that experience. To embrace it. To think, *This is so cool,* as opposed to, *Oh my gosh, this is freaking me out.*

Regardless of your emotions, remember two things. The first is that it's normal to feel this way. It *is* exciting! If you weren't at least a tiny bit intimidated and unsure at your first auction, I'd think there was something wrong with you. So enjoy it. You're fine. Have some fun. If you feel you're really in danger of tilting, do nothing but watch. There will be other days and other auctions.

The second thing is that the other people are just like you. They might have more experience, or they may have less. Regardless, they have a human brain like you and are facing the same uncertainties.

That's one of my favorite things about auctions: For all the money, all the people, all the competition and uncertainty, we are all human. Underneath it all, we're the same.

Sold! To the Person with the Foreclosure Book!

Thanks to your diligence and persistence, one of your visits to auction will pay off. You'll hear the trustee say, "Sold!" and *you'll* be the winning bidder.

It's an exciting moment. It's so validating to work through the process and then win a bid at a price you're confident will allow you to make a profit. It's a real "take control of your life" moment. Enjoy it.

You can proudly walk up to the trustee with your checks in hand and get ready to become a first-time auction buyer!

Then, if you're like me, you might think, *What on earth do I do NOW?*

We've got you covered. Head on to the next chapter, where we itemize each of the critical next steps after a successful bid.

CHAPTER 10
NOW WHAT?
What to Do Immediately After Buying Your First Property

We recently set a new personal record for single-day auction purchases: We bought nineteen houses in one day.

Over the course of my auction career, we've bought hundreds of homes. Still, nineteen in one day was a high-water mark. It represented a lot of legwork, experience, and diligence. We worked hard to buy those homes.

To do it, we needed a system. What I love is that no matter how many homes we buy, we always use the same system outlined in this book. We've built a team, and we continue to refine the system year over year, but the five basic steps have never changed. We build and filter a list, drive by the houses, analyze the numbers, check the title, and then go to auction and bid. That's it.

What doesn't get enough attention in the foreclosure world, however, is what to do *after* you buy a house. (Or nineteen of them, for that matter.)

For that, we have another system. Like our five steps, it's repeatable, it's reliable, and it works, whether you've just bought your first house at auction or your first dozen.

Check the Receipt
After a successful bid, the trustee gives you a receipt. When you receive

that receipt you should immediately do two things: Take a picture of it, and check the details.

The receipt you won't show the property address—don't worry, that's normal—but it will show the borrower's name, the trustee's name, how much you paid for the property at auction, and how much you gave the trustee. It will also indicate the *vesting*, which indicates who will actually own the property. (For example, if you have someone bidding on your behalf at auction or the title of the property will be in a different name than the person bidding, the vesting specifies that.)

Your job is to verify the details. *Be very diligent.* Make sure the numbers are right. Make sure the spelling is correct. Double-check that the check amounts on the receipt match the checks you gave the trustee.

Take your time, and don't feel pressured by the people around you. For the moment, this is the only evidence that you just spent a significant sum of money on a house that you've probably never seen the inside of. These details will also be used to transfer the deed, as well as issue any refund you may be entitled to. (Refunds are common, since most of the time you won't have the exact amount in cashier's checks.) While it is possible to change these details later, it can be time-consuming and difficult. Getting it right the first time is so much easier.

Head to the Property

Hey—congratulations! You just bought a house!

The first thing you'll want to do when you leave the auction is go see your new asset. This is about more than just the sheer excitement of having bought your first property at auction. You'll need to sort out a few details as you can. There are two possible scenarios at your new property: It could be vacant, or it could be occupied (although most will be vacant).

If you plan to sell or renovate the property, vacant is generally better. We're going to run through the steps as if the property is vacant, followed by what to do if it's occupied. The steps are similar, but there are some key differences.

Next Steps for Vacant Properties

If you still aren't sure whether your house is vacant, refer back to the drive-by chapter—there are a number of tips there to help you out.

Even if you are confident that the property is vacant, it's always good policy to knock on the door when you first arrive, just in case. Assuming the place is indeed empty, here are the steps you'll follow. We'll go through each in turn:

1. Gain access and secure the property.
2. Take photos and create your master task and trade list.
3. Contact your insurer.
4. Turn on the utilities.

1. Gain Access and Secure the Property

Your first job on arrival is to gain access and secure the house as your own. You'll rarely have keys to a property, and while it's not uncommon for a vacant home to be unlocked, more often than not you're going to need a locksmith to help you get in. Once you do get access, make sure you or the locksmith do the following:

- **Change/rekey the locks.** Never skip this step. Even if you have keys to existing locks, you have no idea how many keys are out there or who has them, so *do not skip this step.*
- **Add a lockbox.** Once you have your new keys to your new lock, add a lockbox to store a set in. This will be invaluable for access for tradespeople and contractors. It will also save you untold trips to the house as well as the hassle of cutting a pile of extra keys that you'll quickly lose track of.
- **Unplug the garage door opener.** Really. While it rarely happens, a former tenant or owner may still have the remote for the garage door, which can give them access to the house even after you rekey the locks. Simply unplug the opener itself.
- **Secure the windows and doors.** Make sure the windows, patio doors, and any other access points are locked. You can use pieces of wood to secure sliding doors and windows in the short term.

2. Take Photos and Create Your Master Task and Trade List

After securing your new property, it's time to document the condition of the house. This doesn't take long and is extremely useful, for two reasons.

The first is that in the next step, you're going to insure your new property. At the moment, the home is technically uninsured—after all, it just changed ownership. You're the new owner, but because you didn't *know* you were going to be the new owner until auction day, there was no sense in buying insurance in advance. As a result, you're stuck in a bit of a coverage gap. The photos are going to demonstrate the condition of the house on auction day, in the extremely unlikely chance that a disgruntled former owner or tenant crashes their car through the garage door or throws a brick through a window.

(The same rule applies, although to a lesser extent, if the home is occupied. Take as many photos as you can from outside the home, and include any cars in the driveway and their license plates. That will also help in the event of any insurance problems.)

Your photo documentation serves another important purpose. Over the coming weeks you are likely to have a steady stream of trade and service people coming through the property to clean, fix, upgrade, and install everything that's required to rent or sell the property. Your photos—and the notes that you make along the way—are going to be invaluable in organizing the work to be done.

Every contractor has a smartphone. It's easy to send them photos and notes, and have them draw up a quote, lay out a schedule, order materials, and more. Even if you're doing the work yourself, this is the best possible way to stay on top of things and save yourself a huge amount of time in the weeks to come.

As you move through the house, working from outside to inside, take photos and make notes. Some tips:

- Take wide shots of rooms and areas, then close-ups of areas of concern in the same room—things that need repairing or fixing. Going from wide to close-up views in the same room keeps photos grouped together for easier use. Take an overall picture of the master bedroom, for example, followed by a close-up of a broken light switch or a hole in the drywall.
- Don't forget to include photos of HVAC systems, electrical panels, utility meters, and appliances (and note their sizes). You'll use these for insurance and for setting up utilities at a later step. Get photos of the plates/labels that show the model and serial numbers.
- Create a master scope-of-work list as you go, and note the relevant trades: trash removal, paint, HVAC, and so on.
- Check that things *work*—lights, fans, appliances, heating and cooling systems, etc.

Now is the perfect time to do this. Don't wait. Done right, your photo tour and master list will save you innumerable misunderstandings, forgotten to-dos, and unnecessary trips to the property.

> **Note:** You can download our photo-document guide, as well as a scope-of-work template, at **BiggerPockets.com/ForeclosureBonus**.

3. Contact Your Insurer

It's critical to note that you just bought a house that is now *not* insured. One of your first jobs is to fix that.

Many buyers will call their insurance company en route to the house, but often you'll need some of the information you've gathered from your photo tour and inspections.

For the first-time auction buyer, the easiest place to find insurance is through the same provider that handles your home. You'll be a trusted client, the rates will probably be fair, and you can get things happening quickly. You'll also be able to plan the process in advance with them by calling before the auction and asking what the process is for insuring another home.

Vacant property tends to be slightly *more* expensive to insure than occupied property. If you're not yet sure of occupancy, consider it occupied from an insurance perspective. The greatest insurance risk in the short term—and it's not very big—is from an occupant damaging or stealing something after you take possession. Even if they do it by accident, a house that burns to the ground after auction is *your* house. You want it insured.

4. Turn on the Utilities

Now that your property is insured, it's time to get the lights on!

In vacant homes, it's common to find that the utilities have been shut off. As people fall behind on their mortgages, they also tend to fall behind on gas, water, and electricity payments. The utility companies, the lender, or even an HOA board may have shut these off for nonpayment. You're going to want them back on. Not only will you need them to sell or rent the home, but you'll need utilities to effectively make your repairs and upgrades. Typically, this is as easy as calling the respective utility companies. The data from your photo tour, like meter numbers, can sometimes be helpful.

While you're at it, be sure to make calls to any property maintenance services regarding landscaping, grass cutting, and/or gardening. This is particularly important in communities with an HOA and municipalities with regulations about property maintenance. They may be able to impose fines for improper maintenance, and now that the property has a new, solvent owner, that means they can start fining you.

Next Steps for Occupied Properties

When a property is occupied—or you suspect that it is—the order of operations is a little different, and it changes depending on how events unfold.

Insure the Property

The first step, regardless, is to insure the property. **In the vast majority of cases, dealing with the occupants (either tenants or the previous owners) of a foreclosed home goes relatively smoothly.** But bear in mind that these are emotional times for the people living there. Sometimes they don't *know* that the home just changed hands; they may be renters who have no idea. If the occupant is the previous owner, they're not likely to be feeling their best. Your wisest choice is to insure the property as quickly as possible—and *before* you go on to the next step.

Talk to the Occupant

Once the property is insured, the critical next step is to talk to the occupant. The simplest way? Just knock on the door.

If the occupant is home, it's time to introduce yourself.

There's no ideal script or single right way to approach this conversation. Are you looking for a tenant? If so, the perfect one could be standing in front of you. If you're looking to renovate and flip the property, there's a good chance you'd like the person to leave, and that's a different conversation. Whatever the situation, always begin the same way: introduce yourself. "I'm sorry to bother you," I usually say. "My name is Aaron. I'm not sure if you were aware, but this house was scheduled for trustee sale today."

At this point, sometimes you get a nod or a terse yes. Occasionally, you get a shocked look. Very occasionally someone is happy to see you, but most of the time it's not a cheery occasion.

"The company I work for purchased this house at auction today," I typically say. "I came by to reach out and give you my contact information so we can talk about next steps."

Once you've made contact, the critical pieces of information you want to know are:

- **Did the occupant know this was coming?** This question helps you gauge the situation. If this is a shock, they're going to need more time. It also helps to move the conversation forward in a positive way. What you're looking for in *all* cases is a productive conversation. Having some sympathy and understanding for their situation is a great place to start.
- **Is the occupant a tenant or the former owner?** This question helps you determine next steps as well. If the occupant is a tenant, one of the first things we tell them is to not pay the previous landlord any more rent. If they have a legal lease at market value with a third party (as opposed to, say, a dirt-cheap rental from a family member), you'll have to honor that lease—for at least ninety days in many states.
- **Does the occupant have plans for where they are going next?** This is the big one. If they have a plan—and hopefully they do—you can support them. If they don't, they're going to *need* a plan.

In all cases, this is a conversation. You want it to be friendly but firm and clear. Every situation is different. Sometimes people are angry—maybe not at you specifically, but that anger might be directed at you. The best advice I can give is to *listen.* The more empathetic and understanding you can be, the more likely you are to come up with a win-win scenario.

What constitutes a win-win is going to be different every time. More often than not, the outcome you're looking for is that the occupant moves out. Ideally, they do it willingly and quickly.

When we want someone to move faster, we'll do a "cash for keys" deal. There are a few scenarios where this can be helpful. For example:

- The occupants have a lease, but you'd like them to leave so you can sell the place.
- The rent is so low that you need them to leave so you can renovate and bring in higher-paying tenants.
- The occupants are stubborn or difficult, and paying them seems like the best solution.

Regardless, cash for keys is basically paying someone to leave, and there are a couple of things to remember:

- **This is a business decision.** You should be spending the money because it will save or earn you more. Perhaps paying the occupant is cheaper than the eviction process. Maybe it can speed up the flipping process, so you spend less money on financing. Whatever the scenario, do not pay cash for keys unless doing so benefits you.
- **Get it in writing.** Use an agreement, signed by both parties, that states the terms—that you've agreed not to evict them, they've agreed to leave by a certain date, and you've agreed to cover their costs by a specified amount. (You can find a cash-for-keys sample agreement on the resource site.)

If the Occupant Isn't Home

If the occupant doesn't answer the door, your next step is to leave a "hello letter."

The hello letter is a short and polite note. In it, you identify yourself and let the occupant know that you bought the property at auction that day, and ask them to please call you to discuss next steps. Tape it to the door, or tuck it in the door handle. Then:

- Take exterior photos as if the place were unoccupied.
- Knock on neighbors' doors to try to learn more about the occupancy status.
- If you don't hear back from the occupant, return the next day and check to see whether the hello letter is still there.
- If the letter is still there, give the occupant a couple more days. Come back each day and check again.

After three days, if we've had no response from the occupant and the letter is still there, our next step is to call a locksmith and gain access to the property by rekeying the back door.

The reasoning is this: If we do the back door first and discover the place is empty, we can proceed with all the steps we previously outlined that apply to a vacant home. The plan at this point is the same.

If, however, we rekey the back door and it's obvious the place is occupied, we take pictures to show the work we did on the door, then leave and lock the door behind us. Next, we leave a different note on the front door describing what we've done: that we entered the property, found there were still possessions there, and left.

Occasionally, people pass away or simply move and leave all their possessions. In those cases, if you believe there are possessions of value, you're required to store them for a certain amount of time. The rules vary from state to state, but typically, you pay to move the material and store it in a facility for a period during which the owner can reclaim their possessions by paying you the storage and moving fees.

Rekeying the back door when you're not sure whether the place is occupied may seem awkward, but it's a step you have to take. Most of the time you'll already have a good idea of the occupancy status from talking to neighbors and looking around.

Of the thousands of homes I've bought at auction, I've come across only a couple where we rekeyed the back door and were surprised to find it still occupied.

Eviction

Sometimes, people simply won't move on. You might speak with the occupant and they refuse to move out, or the occupant may simply refuse to respond to you at all.

In either case, your next step is to start the eviction process.

Every state has its own rules for eviction, and they can vary widely. Texas and California, for example, have very different approaches to landlord-tenant law. Regardless of where you live, it's best to contact an attorney who specializes in eviction law for the area you're buying in.

You can, and should, do much of this legwork in advance by contacting attorneys to understand the eviction process, including timelines and fees. It's much easier to deal with occupants on things like cash for keys when you know exactly how much the alternative costs. You can also easily find the eviction process information for your county with a quick online search.

Here's an possible scenario for someone who refuses to respond to your request to talk to them:

- You knock on the door. No answer. You leave a hello letter.
- You return a few days later. You leave another hello letter.
- You wait a couple more days, then leave a move-out notice on the door. This is typically a *notice to vacate* the property in three to five days, depending on the state. (Note: Once you've had an attorney

prepare this document, you can prepare one yourself using the same language if you need another in the future.)

- At this point, we find that about half of occupants will call—they know you're getting serious. When they do, you can have the conversation you wanted to have if they had just answered the door in the first place.
- If they don't respond to the notice to vacate, you move on with eviction proceedings according to local law. Typically, the eviction has to be granted or approved by a judge. Then the eviction date is scheduled with a sheriff or constable. They'll place a notice on the door a few days prior to the eviction date that lets the occupants know they'll be forcibly removed if they are still there.

This can take anywhere from a few weeks to a few months, depending on the law, the courts, and local law enforcement.

Of the many evictions we've done, only three or four times have people refused to leave on their own after receiving the notice to vacate. At that point, they know things are serious. Typically, you'll arrive at the house with the sheriff to find it already vacant.

Bring a locksmith with you—law enforcement won't gain you entry to the house. The locksmith changes the locks, and the sheriff or constable will go through the house to make sure it's safe and empty. At that point, *the property is yours.* Call the insurance company to change that status from occupied to vacant. Then you can start the process you'd normally go through with a vacant property—securing the house, taking photos, and so on.

The occupants may have left belongings, in which case you'll have to schedule a time for them to claim their items if they wish. Depending on the state, your timeline, and the amount of stuff, you may have to pay to move it to storage.

Eviction is something you can usually do almost entirely on your own, with the exception of the local sheriff or constable coming to the house to ensure that the occupants leave. Whether you choose to perform all the necessary steps yourself or use an attorney to help is up to you. Like many other decisions, it's based on time and money, and how much you want to spend of each.

Eviction is a worst-case scenario; no one wants it. It's expensive and time-consuming, so you're usually better off paying someone to move, simply to speed things up and cut overall costs.

The Night of the Auction: Partner Update

The evening of the day you buy your property is a great time for one last administrative task. If you have partners, investors, or lenders, send out a celebratory email to update them—after all, you've got great news!

Put the property address in the subject line, and in the body of the email, give them the details of the transaction, including how much you paid, the refund expected, and any relevant information you obtained from securing the property and speaking with the occupants.

It's a moment to celebrate and an excellent time to capture the details of the day. It also positions you as an effective steward for investment partners. Investors love someone who is organized and communicative. Be that person.

A Week (or So) Later: Title Recording

About a week after your successful bid at auction, you should receive two things: the deed to the property and your refund, if you have one coming. The refund is any amount left from the cashier's checks at auction.

The refund is always nice to get back; the deed is critical.

What you receive on the day of auction is just a receipt. It acknowledges that you've bought something. But technically, what you've really bought is someone's unpaid *debt*. Loans are foreclosed on, not properties. After a few days, the trustee who sold you that foreclosed loan will send you a trustee's deed. That document stipulates the property is being transferred from the prior owner to the new owner, *you*.

Here's the important part. Although the deed has your name on it and is a legal document, many times it hasn't officially been recorded anywhere yet. The deed is simply a document from a lawyer's office that's been sent to you. The tax records haven't been updated. The utility records haven't been updated. As far as they're concerned, the *previous* owner is still the owner of record. As soon as you receive the trustee's deed in the mail, it's time to make one last run to the county recorder's office to record the transfer.

- Double-check the deed. Make sure the details and the spelling are 100 percent accurate.
- In some areas, the deed you receive will already be recorded. Check yours—it should indicate whether it's recorded or unrecorded. Recorded deeds may take longer to arrive. Although you won't have

to take them to the county clerk to record them, you still have to check them carefully for errors.

- Don't drag your heels. In theory, there's a gray area between when you buy the property at auction and when the deed is recorded. In the unlikely event that someone files a lawsuit during that period, things can get messy. Promptly recording your deed is just good policy.
- If you find errors in the deed or don't receive your deed or refund, go back to the auction receipt, and call the office of the trustee who sold the foreclosure to you to resolve the errors.

Once you've recorded the deed and deposited your check, you're done. You've finalized your ownership of the property. Congratulations!

Disclose, Disclose, Disclose

If you're investing in foreclosures in order to renovate and then resell properties, there's one important thing to remember.

A good Realtor will tell you to always disclose any uncertainties, past troubles, or oddities on any property you sell. This is particularly true with properties bought at auction. In the world of foreclosures, you're selling something you've never lived in, set foot in, or in cases like ours, something you've never even *seen*. Not only that, but you're clearly buying a property that has a less-than-typical past, one that you often know very little about.

All these things combine to create a situation ripe for blowback *unless you disclose them.*

In other words, if you're flipping the house you just bought at auction, *don't hide that fact.* Disclose everything you know, including how you purchased the house.

Disclose, disclose, disclose!

The Elephant in the Room

Let's take a look at the big picture of our process so far. At this point, you know everything you need to know to analyze, bid on, and buy a house at auction. You know how to keep your cool at auction, how to take possession of the house after a successful bid, and how to take care of the final details to ensure the property is yours to do with as you see fit.

So what's stopping you?

For many people, there's one final barrier. It's the elephant in the room that we've been studiously ignoring: *Auctions take cash.*

What if you don't have any?

It's a reasonable question. Most people don't have six figures in extra cash just lying around. How do you get into a business that requires such a large up-front investment?

Fear not. If that's the scenario you're facing, you're far from alone. And there are more solutions than you might realize.

The time has come to talk about money.

CHAPTER 11
MONEY

Or, What to Do When You Don't Have Any

I was fortunate enough to learn the auction business in a low-risk way. I bought my first few properties when I was working for another company. Technically, the money we were spending at auction was theirs, not mine. I still lost plenty of sleep over those early decisions—using other people's money doesn't mean you don't care—but to be sure, it was less risky than using my own.

After our first trip to auction, I managed to buy four more houses at the courthouse with the company I was working for. I was getting paid a salary to do it, but it wasn't a lot. I began to wonder, *Why can't I do this on my own?*

The answer, of course, was always the same: *Because I don't have any money.*

Things changed when my wife and I were expecting our second child.

At the time, my wife was working nights as a waitress at a casino to help make ends meet. I'd come home from work at six, she'd hand me our kid, and then she'd go to work until two in the morning.

It was a draining schedule for any family, but things had gotten tougher with my wife's pregnancy. Not only was she on her feet all night, but she was also exhausted and sleeping very little.

The hardest part was that the whole crazy arrangement wasn't even solving our financial problems. For all our hard work and sacrifice, we were still losing ground every week, slipping further into debt as each month passed. Something had to change.

Change arrived on one of those long nights at the casino.

During one of her shifts, my wife went into labor. It was early—six *weeks* early. The baby was safe, but it was a turning point for all of us.

I remember looking at my new daughter, separated from all of us by the walls of an incubator, and thinking, *This can't go on.* I was certain that the difficulty of shift work and our stressful financial situation had been responsible for the premature birth.

Right then, I made a decision to move on.

I would start my own company. I would invest in foreclosures at auction. I would take what I'd learned on those first houses and use it to make a better life for my family.

I handed in my resignation the next day.

There was just one catch, of course: We were broke. In fact, we were worse than broke. And I'd just abandoned our only source of income to go into a business that required investing six figures at a time in *cash*.

The Cash Barrier

Buying foreclosures on the courthouse steps is first and foremost a cash business. With some exceptions, you need to pay in full for the property you buy almost immediately.

To make the problem thornier, it's difficult to borrow money from traditional sources to buy at auction. You might be able to get a mortgage for a house you buy on the open market, but that all changes at the courthouse.

Most banks and other traditional mortgage lenders need an appraisal or a home inspection before they're willing to provide a loan. Because appraisers and inspectors can't actually get inside to see the place, you likely won't have much luck there.

Still, people are buying at auction every week. How are they doing it?

Broke and Buying at Auction

That was where I found myself. Broke, unemployed, and with a new baby in an incubator, I was in debt and so overwhelmed that at times I could barely function.

And yet, I'd decided to go into a cash-only business that banks don't really want to touch. Was I crazy?

The answer to that question, I realized, didn't matter. For months, I'd been telling myself I didn't have the cash to go into business. I no longer had that luxury. I'd burned my bridges. I *had* to succeed.

With traditional borrowing off the table, the first person I approached was my dad. I came to him with a proposition: If he provided the cash, I would do everything else. I'd do the research and drive by the houses. I'd bid at auction. And at the end, I'd sell the house for him and give him all the profit.

What would I get? I'd get the commission as a sales agent. I'd also get something more important: the chance to go back to auction and do what I really wanted to.

It worked. My dad agreed to the deal. I found our first place at auction and was able to sell it not long after. Then I did another. Then another. It was working!

My dad and I went on to do eight or ten houses together, and over time, the deal began to shift. Instead of my receiving just the sales commission at the end, we transitioned into a partnership and split the profits. For the first time in my life, I was being rewarded based on my performance. Better still, I felt like I was in control; we weren't quite out of the financial quicksand yet, but we were making progress, and that progress was in my hands.

It wasn't long before things shifted again. My dad had been telling other people about the success we were having, and soon enough someone in his network approached me. Suddenly, I had *two* investors! Back to auction I went, and this time I was able to buy four houses at once.

Within a few months, word had spread a little more, and I found myself giving a presentation to an investor group. That increased our capital even more.

Within a year or two, I was one of the largest foreclosure buyers in Northern California.

At the time, I was struck not only by how fast things had changed but by how little I had previously understood the financial side of auction. I had spent months and months wanting to go to auction on my own but remained frozen for lack of capital.

All that time I'd been incapable of seeing the fundamental truth: I didn't *need* to have money to buy at auction. I could use other people's money—and there were plenty of other people.

LESSON: You need money to buy at auction. But you don't need *your* money.

The Reality of Foreclosure Finance

Here's where I do my Wizard of Oz routine and pull back the curtain to reveal the reality of foreclosures. It might be the most important part of this book.

> **Most of the people at auction don't have the cash to be at auction.**

It's true. They don't. Trust me, I know. Not only have I been there, but I meet those people every week, and they tell me. They don't have six figures in cash lying around to bid on a house. Most of them don't even have four figures.

Yet they're still buying houses.

That's right. Most of the people buying houses at auction are doing it the same way I did: with other people's money.

When you're short on cash, it can be hard to believe that other people are struggling with an *excess* of the stuff, but trust me, it's true. There's an unbelievable abundance of capital in the world, and one of the thorniest problems for the people who have it is how to put it to productive use.

Your job is to find those people and show them how.

Two Degrees of Kevin Bacon

Six degrees of separation is the idea that everyone is six or fewer social connections apart. It was popularized in the form of Six Degrees of Kevin Bacon, a game where you compete with other players to discover the smallest number of connections between a given actor and Kevin Bacon.

What goes for Bacon goes for you and auctions. Only in your case, the odds are even better. There's only one Kevin Bacon in the world, but there are thousands of people close to your network with the cash to buy at auction. Right now, in fact, you are almost certainly just two or three degrees of separation from the money required to bid on the courthouse steps.

Which leads us to two questions. How do you find those people? And how do you convince them that *you're* the person they should partner with?

1. Finding Potential Investors

Connecting with someone who has the money to fund your auction plans begins with identifying the people who are just *one* degree of separation away—the people you actually know or have met.

I found it easiest to start this process with a good old-fashioned list. Start generating names of people you can talk to about your plans. To help jog your memory, here are some possibilities:

- Bankers
- Mortgage brokers and mortgage company employees
- Accountants
- Financial advisors
- Real estate professionals
- Property appraisers
- Contractors and tradespeople
- Family
- Friends
- Coworkers

In the beginning, I took my list and started by reaching out to the people I felt most comfortable having a conversation with. In my case, that was my friends and family.

On the surface, this looks like typical networking, and to be clear, it is. But there's a deeper truth here that you should pay attention to: Most people that can connect you to the money you need are also the people you encounter during the five steps.

That means that one of the best networking tools at your disposal is to simply start working the process. In fact, I can almost guarantee that you'll make new connections while working your way through the five steps. And each connection is one connection closer to your future financial partner.

For example:

- If you go to a bank to ask about financing, they might refer you to an alternative lender, like a mortgage broker. That broker might connect you with a real estate investor.
- If you ask a real estate agent about broker price opinions, they might refer you to a client who just downsized their home and is looking for an investment.
- If you ask a contractor about renovation costs, they might decide they want to be your construction partner and split the upfront costs of auction.

The trick to all these conversations is to *talk about what you're doing.* You don't just ask the plumber what it costs to swap out the dishwasher; you tell them why you're asking. You don't just ask the agent if they can help with valuation; you tell them why you're asking.

Tell people you're planning on buying at auction. Be honest. Tell them you're analyzing properties and looking for investors. It's that easy. Eventually, the trail that begins with your network is going to lead you to the partner you're looking for.

> **LESSON:** You have a great network already. Activate it by (a) working the five steps and (b) talking about what you're doing.

2. Selling Your Plan

When you find a potential investor, you have two primary jobs ahead of you. The first is to convince them that investing in foreclosed homes is a good financial choice. Your best tool for that job is data—specifically, hard numbers on auction results.

Fortunately, gathering this data is free and relatively easy to do. Plus, you'll get to learn while you build the evidence to back up your plan.

As always, start working the steps of the process *even if you don't have the money.* Pull the listing data. Drive by the houses. Analyze the properties. Then go to auction just as if you were going to bid.

Instead of bidding, however, you're going to take note of an opening bid and what that property ultimately goes for. Then you're going to keep an eye on that property, revisiting it online. Once it sells, you now have a business case, since you can estimate the return on that house. Do that for ten houses, and you'll have some real numbers: auction price, resale price, time to sell, profit, rate of return.

This is exactly how I convinced my dad to invest with me for the very first time. Later, when I had the opportunity to pitch a small hedge fund out of Tahoe, I did the same thing again. This time I had even more data, and because it was based on houses I'd sold myself, it was even more accurate.

Your second job, once you've gathered the evidence that investing in foreclosures is a solid financial choice, is to convince investors that *you* are the right person for the job.

Bringing them the numbers is a big first step. Most people who have the money to invest have also developed the financial literacy to understand that every investment needs a return.

Your data will demonstrate that, but it will also reveal another characteristic that investors prize: a methodical, repeatable approach to making money. Showing your exact process—the same five-step process in this book—will also help.

Don't be afraid to showcase "your" unique process for profiting in the foreclosure business. You have our permission to brag.

Creating a Financial Arrangement

Once you have a backer, you'll need to come up with an arrangement. What does your financial partner get in exchange for their money? How do you create a fair agreement that reflects what each party is bringing to the table?

Here are several common arrangements we see at auction. Again, remember that the majority of buyers out there aren't using their own money. They've come up with creative ways to reward each other for becoming partners.

Profit Split

Probably the most common type of arrangement I see is a simple profit-sharing agreement. The investor provides the cash; the buyer provides the legwork and experience. After the house is sold, they split the profits on a predetermined basis.

What does that split look like? It can be anything you want. Generally, it'll depend on the experience of you, the auction buyer. Early on, you'll have limited experience, which means you're bringing less to the table and the risk is higher for the investor. In that case, you might get only 25 percent of the profits. Later, when you have a track record, you can rightfully cut a deal for more.

That said, there are a lot of 50/50 deals out there. It's simple and it often feels like the fairest arrangement.

Skill Partnering

As you now know, buying at auction requires a broad range of skills, many of which are quite valuable on the open market.

If you have skilled trade or contracting experience, for example, that can be a valuable contribution to a partnership. You provide the labor, time, and perhaps the funds to get the home ready to sell, while your financial partner provides the cash at auction. When you sell, you split any profits according to your particular arrangement.

The same can apply if you have extensive real estate experience or legal skills. Your experience is worth something to the right person in the right situation.

Financing

Because the timelines are tight and complete property inspections aren't possible, banks and mortgage brokers are typically unable to lend cash for auction purchases. But that doesn't mean a private lender can't help.

A lender can provide you with cashier's checks for the auction under prearranged terms similar to those for a typical mortgage (although the rates are likely to be higher). There can be many variations, including short-term borrowing fees just for using the money while you find traditional financing after auction, or more traditional profit sharing, based on an agreed split. The possibilities are almost endless.

Fee for Service

Some people get paid to go to auction; others get paid to do the construction work on a house that's been bought at auction. They might also get a small share of future profits.

It's similar to the arrangement I had with my dad. He provided the capital; I supplied the auction services and got to keep the sales commission at the end for acting as the selling agent. There was no profit in it for me, but that changed over time.

In these types of deals you may not get much, if any, ownership, but doing auction work for a fee can get you into the game, and you can grow from there, the same way I did.

Auction Financing

Increasingly, we're seeing lenders that specifically serve the auction buying market.

Those lenders, however, still face the same challenges that traditional lenders do when it comes to auction. There's no title insurance. There's no professional inspection. There's little time and a lot of unknowns.

Expect, then, that companies providing this service are either going to demand a track record—solid credit or some auction experience—or charge high fees/rates to borrow money. Or both.

Aligned Incentives

There are as many ways to do deals as there are deals to be done. Here's what we've learned—mostly the hard way—about all of them: The best arrangements, the best partnerships, and the best collaborations happen when incentives are aligned. In other words, if getting a great deal at auction is what *you* need to succeed, your partner should want the same thing. If your partner wins only if you lose, or wins more if you lose, or wins no matter what, the incentives are misaligned. Not all these scenarios are deal breakers, but they're definitely not optimal.

Let's look at a few examples.

- **Scenario 1.** You have a financial backer. They put up the money, you contribute the auction work and knowledge, and you both win by splitting the profits on the sale of the house. Those are aligned incentives. You both lose if the deal fails, and you both win if the deal is successful.
- **Scenario 2.** You have a financial backer. They loan you the money, and you pay them interest. In this case, you win only if you can buy a property and then rent or sell it at a profit. Your backer wins either way since you have to make the loan payments regardless. They may win a *little* more when you turn a profit because you're more likely to make the loan payments if you do, but your incentives are certainly *less aligned.*
- **Scenario 3.** You get paid to do the renovations on a house purchased at auction. Your partner fronts you the cash. In this case, you're getting paid no matter what, while your partner is taking some speculative risks. Your incentives are *less aligned.*

The Trick to Auction Money: Just Start

It took a life-changing event to get me started in my own auction business, and I wouldn't change a thing.

But you don't need that kind of drama to make things happen. The trick is to just *start*. Work through all five steps.

Once I asked for money, I found it. But I'd wasted months and months thinking about how I didn't have any money, not realizing I could just use someone else's. It was only absolute necessity that got me going.

My advice would be to skip that step!

When I finally got started, I went to the courthouse and bought foreclosures at auction for almost two years before using any of my own money. I purchased dozens of houses that way. Then, when I was on better financial footing, I started reinvesting my excess capital the same way.

Looking back, the larger lesson is one that I've now heard over and over from the wealthiest people I know: *Opportunity and money find each other.*

A great real estate deal and money are a little like the opposite poles of a magnet: They attract each other. If you can find a deal at the courthouse, you'll find the money to take with you.

LESSON: Find a deal and the money will find you.

Work the steps, and use them as a way to network. Just start!

CHAPTER 12
YOUR FIRST COURTHOUSE STEP
Getting Comfortable and Getting Started

If this book is your introduction to real estate in general or to foreclosure auctions in particular, it's easy to feel overwhelmed by all there is to know and do.

That's normal. *Everyone* was a beginner at some point. The best advice I can offer you is this: When things start to feel like too much, simply take your time and trust the process.

Right now, your job is simply to *start*. The least overwhelming way to do that is to remember that you don't have to buy anything; you can take just a single, small step.

There's nothing stopping you from looking at foreclosure notices online or building a spreadsheet. There's no reason you can't have an enjoyable afternoon drive by a property on your way home from work. No one can stop you from taking a peek at Google Maps or visiting Zillow for some sales data. You're welcome to look up public county records and read the loan documents.

With that in mind, consider some of the simple steps that follow. They're all virtually free to do, they entail no risk, and they'll help you transition out of uncertainty and discomfort.

1. Sign up for free access to our resource page. You'll get access to sample spreadsheets, agreements, and checklists for every step in

the book. Just visit Biggerpockets.com/ForeclosureBonus.

2. Visit sites like Realtor.com, Zillow, or some of the others listed in the resources, and start by searching out your *own* home on the big real estate sites. Let that be your first project! It can be the first listing on your spreadsheet.

3. Take a stab at valuing one or two properties that have sold, *without* looking at their sales history. You can then check your work by looking at the actual sale price to see how close you came.

4. Attend an auction. Why not? It's free, it's fun, and there's no purchase necessary!

Four easy steps. You can do them whenever you want, in any order—comfortably and safely, without spending a dime.

So be curious, and take a few small steps. Create your own "Foreclosure College," and grant yourself an honorary doctorate. Consider this book your undergraduate degree.

But never forget: *Risk and reward are conjoined twins.* There will come a time when being comfortable and safe won't take you any further. There will come a time when you need to leave Foreclosure College and head out into the big, brave world of The Real Thing.

For now, though, just begin. Take a baby step. And really—go to an auction. It's more fun than you might imagine.

Dip your toes in the water. You might like it.

And when you're ready to swim? When you've got your strokes down, and you're ready to toss away the life preserver?

Then go for it.

The Other Upside

Foreclosures are never fun.

No one—not the homeowner, the lender, the county, or the trustees—really *wants a* foreclosure to happen.

Still, the business gets a bad rap at times. The story people like to tell is that an unfortunate soul fell on hard times, and the greedy bank took their house and forced them out on the street.

The people like you who want to buy foreclosed properties are sometimes painted with the same negative brush. Even though you didn't borrow the money, you didn't loan the money, and you didn't foreclose on the home, it can still feel as if you're doing something wrong. "Profiting from someone's misfortune" is what some people call it.

That's an easy story to fall for and become angry about. But it's just a story. Foreclosures happen for many reasons, and they're not always about the bank or the economy or greed.

Last year we purchased a home at auction, one of many that year. We knew the home was still occupied, and one of our first jobs, as always, was to stop by the property and talk to the occupants. Ideally, I wanted them to stay on as tenants.

This is always a tricky moment. You can never be sure how people will respond. In fact, even though I know better, I still sometimes secretly hope that no one is home so I can just leave a note and walk away.

This time, that's exactly what happened. As on so many other days, I tucked a note in the door explaining the situation and got back in my car. There were more houses to see, more doors to knock on.

Later that night, I received the following email:

Dear Aaron,

Thank you so much for reaching out to my husband and me! You have made an extremely difficult and awful situation much easier for us. My husband and I would be thrilled to stay in this house. The rent is just fine with us.

We appreciate you working with us. You let me know what you need done and we will do whatever you need.

Thank you again for your kindness and patience.

These are the stories you don't hear about in the foreclosure business. Stories where someone falls on hard times and then someone like you buys their home at auction and lets them stay on as a tenant. Someone like you, in other words, helps them get back on their feet—and maybe even helps them buy back their home.

There are stories about homes that have been empty for years—until someone like you comes along and cleans up the property, renovates the house, and then rents or sells it to new owners. Those are the times when the neighbors come by and shake your hand, offer their tools or their lawnmower, or even pick up a shovel and pitch in.

There are times, in other words, when foreclosures, as tough as they may be, end in *gratitude*.

It's not always easy to buy a house on the courthouse steps. And even when you do buy one, it's not always easy afterward. But that's the point: If it were easy, everyone would do it. And you're not everyone. That's why there's money to be made at auction, and why *you* can make it.

In our worldview, that's why there's also good to be done.

We think of auction as the turnaround point. It's when the pain of the homeowner, the pain of the lender, and the pain of everyone else who may have suffered through the process finally begins to turn the corner. People get repaid. Homes get repaired. Wounds begin to heal.

Buying at auction might be difficult at times, but that doesn't mean you aren't doing something positive.

Here's to your first day at the courthouse. May it be a successful one, and the first of many more.

ACKNOWLEDGMENTS

By now, you know how much we value a team approach to finding profit on the courthouse steps. We've always believed in surrounding yourself with great people who are the best at what they do, and this book is no exception. Behind the names on the cover is a long list of amazing people who contributed to this project.

First of all, thank you to our families. When we started in this business, my wife used to stand at auction while holding our baby, then hop in the car and drive the next round of houses. David and I both have countless stories like these—examples of how our families supported us time and again in our real estate journey. It's an understatement to say we couldn't have done any of this without you.

Our gratitude also goes out to our early investors (you know who you are). You took a greater risk than many, and I still believe you did it less with an eye for high returns, and more because you saw something in us that you believed in. That kind of faith came at a time when we truly needed it. Thank you.

A huge thank-you to the team at BiggerPockets who not only made this book possible, but have inspired legions of people to follow their real estate dreams: Brandon Turner, David Green, Joshua Dorkin, Scott Trench, Katie Miller, Kaylee Pratt, Wendy Dunning, Louise Collazo, and everyone else who touched this project and helped to get the word out.

Special thanks to Matt King, our right hand who kept this project (and many, many other things) on the rails, and to our collaborative writer Dan Clements, who shaped our experiences and words into the final manuscript.

Finally, to our business teams who supported us along the way and gave us the space we needed to make this happen: thank you for this, and for all you continue to do!

More from
BiggerPockets Publishing

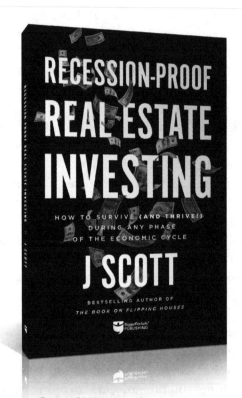

Recession-Proof Real Estate Investing

Take any recession in stride, and never be intimidated by a market shift again. In this book, accomplished investor J Scott dives into the theory of economic cycles and the real-world strategies for harnessing them to your advantage. With clear instructions for every type of investor, this easy-to-follow guide will show you how to make money during all of the market's twists and turns—whether during an economic recession or at any other point in the economic cycle. You'll never look at your real estate business the same way again!

If you enjoyed this book, we hope you'll take a moment to check out some of the other great material BiggerPockets offers. BiggerPockets is the real estate investing social network, marketplace, and information hub, designed to help make you a smarter real estate investor through podcasts, books, blog posts, videos, forums, and more. Sign up today—it's free! **Visit www.BiggerPockets.com.**

The Book on Negotiating Real Estate

When the real estate market gets hot, it's the investors who know the ins and outs of negotiating who will get the deal. J Scott, Mark Ferguson, and Carol Scott combine real-world experience and the science of negotiation in order to cover all aspects of the negotiation process and maximize your chances of reaching a profitable deal.

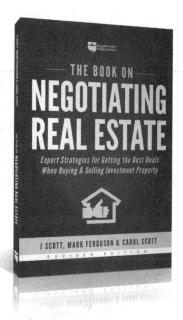

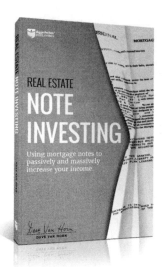

Real Estate Note Investing

Are you a wholesaler, a rehabber, a landlord, or even a turnkey investor? *Real Estate Note Investing* will help you turn your focus to the "other side" of real estate investing, allowing you to make money without tenants, toilets, and termites! Investing in notes is the easiest strategy to earn passive income. Learn the ins and out of notes as investor Dave Van Horn shows you how to get started—and find huge success—in the powerful world of real estate notes!

More from
BiggerPockets Publishing

The Book on Investing in Real Estate with No (and Low) Money Down

Is lack of money holding you back from real estate success? It doesn't have to! In this groundbreaking book from Brandon Turner, author of *The Book on Rental Property Investing*, you'll discover numerous strategies investors can use to buy real estate using other people's money. You'll learn the top strategies that savvy investors are using to buy, rent, flip, or wholesale properties at scale!

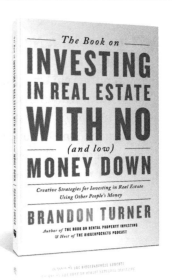

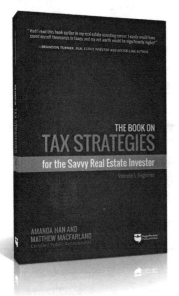

The Book on Tax Strategies for the Savvy Real Estate Investor

Taxes! Boring and irritating, right? Perhaps. But if you want to succeed in real estate, your tax strategy will play a huge role in how fast you grow. A great tax strategy can save you thousands of dollars a year. A bad strategy could land you in legal trouble. That's why BiggerPockets is excited to introduce *The Book on Tax Strategies for the Savvy Real Estate Investor*! You'll find ways to deduct more, invest smarter, and pay far less to the IRS!

Buy, Rehab, Rent, Refinance, Repeat

Invest in real estate and never run out of money! In *Buy, Rehab, Rent, Refinance, Repeat*, you'll discover the incredible strategy known as BRRRR—a long-hidden secret of the ultra-rich and those with decades of experience. Author and investor David Greene holds nothing back, sharing the exact systems and processes he used to scale his business from buying two houses per year to buying two houses per *month* using the BRRRR strategy.

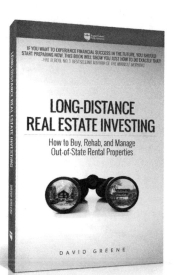

Long-Distance Real Estate Investing

Don't let your location dictate your financial freedom: Live where you want, and invest anywhere it makes sense! The rules, technology, and markets have changed: no longer are you forced to invest only in your backyard. In *Long-Distance Real Estate Investing*, you'll learn an in-depth strategy for building profitable rental portfolios through buying, managing, and flipping out-of-state properties from real estate investor and agent David Greene.

CONNECT WITH BIGGERPOCKETS

and Become Successful in Your Real Estate Business Today!

Facebook
/BiggerPockets

Instagram
@BiggerPockets

Twitter
@BiggerPockets

LinkedIn
/company/Bigger
Pockets

Website
BiggerPockets.com